"Everything you won't find in a US Soccer handbook"
– Eric Wynalda

Re-Booting
Youth Soccer
2.0

The Guide To Running A Soccer Team
From The Original Voice Of The English
Premier League

Re-Booting
Youth Soccer
2.0

*Everything You Really Need to Know But
Were Afraid to Ask About Youth Soccer*

NICK WEBSTER

Be Great Everyday

[signature]

3

Re-Booting Youth Soccer 2.0

Everything You Really Need to Know But Were Afraid to Ask About Youth Soccer

First printing, 2016

ISBN 13: 978-1540437150
ISBN 10: 1540437159

Books may be purchased in quantity by contacting the author, Nick Webster, by email at nick@nickwebsternow.com

To request a speaking engagement, contact the author at nick@nickwebsternow.com

DEDICATION & THANKS

To my coaching mentor Bill Songhurst, who makes me laugh
with stories of how the game used to be played.

To the coaches of the NSCAA, Dr. Robinson, Paul, Jeffrey, Joe
and the lad from Liverpool, Andrew, thanks for developing the
course that paved the way for this book.

To Tyrone, you know why...

To Brian Lofrumento, the most driven twenty-something I've
ever met. Thanks for kicking my butt everyday.

To London, my own little Messi – just be you and try your best in
everything you do.

And to Birchy, you are the rock and foundation of everything I
do. I love you.

A Message From Eric Wynalda
(former US Men's National Team striker 1990-2000)

The world of soccer (football) can be a gloriously misunderstood place when I consider my own journey in its own right. It has without a doubt contained just enough twists and turns to make my life in this game many things.

I have met more than my fair share of fascinating characters, some of which to this day I try to distance myself from – even though our paths had crossed decades ago and our relationship may have been short lived.

Some I still try to stay in contact with, reminiscing, sharing stories that still make us laugh, and usually find that they fall into the "do you really believe that happened" file and then, of course, there are those friends that you do develop long lasting relationships with and you consider them true friends.

With those friends, you try and figure out a way to make sure that they're in your daily dialogue simply because you love or respect them – and if you're lucky, both. Which brings me to the subject matter at heart... let me introduce you to one of my favorite people in football and the world, Nick Webster.

Nick and I knew each other long before we actually met. But we eventually did sit down together at a Coffee Bean in Brentwood, and that is where our friendship began. Let me start by saying that I'm not the easiest to win over and that my disappointment in people in many of my experiences has made me quite jaded. My trust is something that usually takes quite some time to win. Nick won it very quickly as simply put he is one of the most honest, blunt, opinionated, clever, and intuitive people I have ever met, and although his youth might dictate otherwise, he is a great decision maker... what can we say, we were only young once!

On top of that he is a loving father and as a father of six myself it is a quality that I truly admire. I love how he has been able to integrate fatherhood in the sport that he and I love, and that is one reason why I seek his advice to this day.

This is why I would strongly recommend you to read the following pages of this book and to take advantage of what I would call "the real stuff" that matters as you begin or continue your journey in this fascinating sport that Nick and I have spent hundreds of hours talking about.

Over the years it took some time to learn that the noise and the nonsense involved in soccer, especially at the youth level, can be quite a detriment to anyone's learning process. This coming from a guy who grew up with ADHD and severe dyslexia.

My struggle has been harder than most, but without hesitation, I would say read Nick's words and follow his advice. The simplicity and message of "Re-Booting Youth Soccer 2.0" will help you navigate a path that will make the road much smoother.

Nick has been involved in youth soccer at the club and high school level his entire career and he knows what works and doesn't. As a broadcaster, he helped define the English Premier League to a brand new audience and as my producer on the UEFA Champions League show, he developed a platform where I – for better or worse – could be myself without judgment.

Finally, as my partner (not assistant) with Cal FC and for a brief but incredible night with the Atlanta Silverbacks, Nick has helped rewrite the record books and history in the US Open Cup. Our adventures in this legendary competition will probably never be matched and remain to this day the proudest moment in my coaching career.

Nick has succeeded in soccer at so many levels in this country and Re-Booting Youth Soccer 2.0 is just the tool needed to take the game to the next stage of development.

Eric Wynalda
November 7, 2016

Table of Contents

Mission Statement

"I am Nick Webster. I coach and am so passionate about soccer because I believe it is the greatest sport in the world. I know that I make a difference in the lives of people because of the love that I have around this game. I will study, learn and teach everything I can about soccer as a person and a coach. I will aim to be the best that I can be every single day."

This book is just getting started, however, I'd like you to put it down for a minute and think about **your** mission statement. Ask the questions "who am I?" and "what do I stand for?" We all need a mission statement as it helps guide us to the path in what we believe in and who we are.

Core Values

My core values that I teach and follow every day are teamwork, integrity, and hard work.

Like a mission statement, we all need core values. You don't have to have many, but you must believe in and honor your values. They represent who you are, and the players' lives that you touch with these values will pass them down as they grow and interact with the world.

Introduction

Hi – my name is Nick Webster, and for much of the 2000s I was known as the "voice of the English Premier League in the United States." I was the voice that introduced the game with 30-second teases that sounded something like this...

"Arsenal have been firing on all cylinders as they put four past Chelsea and five past City in their last two matches. With Thierry Henry unstoppable, the Professor, Arsene Wenger, is dreaming of Premier League glory, however, United and their canny manager Sir Alex Ferguson know that a win at the Emirates and the title is back up for grabs. Rooney and co are smelling blood...

"It's the Premier League, Arsenal versus Manchester United and it's next on Fox Soccer."

I'd then announce the line-ups before handing it over to the likes of Martin Tyler (who by the way is a smashing fellow). He would call the game until I picked it back up at half-time and full-time to run through the highlights. Yes, it was a dream job. Get paid to watch and talk about my favorite sport, soccer.

Before I knew it, I was off covering World Cups in South Korea/Japan '02, Germany '06, and South Africa '10, as well as the Euros, Portugal '04 and Switzerland/Austria '08, which led to my hosting Fox Football Fone-In with former US international and all round soccer provocatuer, Eric Wynalda.

They were great times and I definitely got my 10,000+ hours of dedicated soccer (see Malcolm Gladwell) while talking to the best players and managers in the world. Yep, the phrase "living the dream" usually popped up with a picture of me, grinning from ear-to-ear.

But let me step back, 40+ years, to where it all began on "The Green," a small field in the village of Ashwell in Hertfordshire, England. It was there as a six-year-old I remember my first game for the school team and scoring nine! As a goal scorer that would be as good as it got, but there is no doubt that that is where the addiction to this game began.

Fast forward a few years… I was living in Sao Paulo, Brazil in spitting distance of the famed Estadio do Morumbi. The year was 1972, and Brazilian football was at the peak of the Samba Boys. The 1970 world champions, Pele, Rivelino, Gerson, and Jairzinho all played in my backyard. I got to sit on the concrete bowl that was the Morumbi with over 100,000 screaming, singing, and dancing fans. Yep, even as an eight-year-old, I was "living the dream."

Two years later I found myself in North London (England), standing on more concrete, this time terracing, at White Hart Lane. Now the names were Chivers, Peters, and Jennings, not quite as glamorous, and neither was the football… but in its own way, it was just as revered and passionate.

It was back in England where I swapped the silky moves of a number 10 to an "up and at them" number 4 (center-back). Gone were the days of taking players on and instead the shout was

"Webster, bloody get rid of it, lump it my son," which of course I did as the coach is always right ... right!!!

I was on course to play non-league football (I definitely wasn't good enough for the pros) having appeared for my school, club, Borough (Harrow), and County (Middlesex) when on a cold and rainy day (is there any other kind in England?), I broke both the tibia and fibula in my left leg challenging a goalkeeper one-on-one. He was twenty-eight and I was sixteen, playing men's football on one of the 88 full sized pitches that were marked out on Hackney Marshes.

I remember clearly laying at the top of the 18 yard box, glancing down at my left leg that was now shaped like an L bracket, thinking, "this doesn't look good" before going into shock. It took the bloody ambulance an hour to find me as there were so many matches going on at the same time – remember, this is well before cell phones as someone had to run off and find a phone box to call 999!

So that was the end of any dreams I had of playing at a decent level. I did, however, come back after a couple of years and still to this day rumble around a local league occasionally reliving those teenage years where I was actually a decent player.

In 1987 I made the decision to leave the rain and gray skies of England and moved to the sunny blue skies of Southern California. Soccer wasn't exactly booming at this juncture in the US, in fact, it was nigh on impossible to find any news, let alone a game on TV, however, I did run into an English coach and legend in Southern California soccer called Norm Jackson.

Norm was an absolute gem who helped found the American Youth Soccer Organization in the 1960s and is a member of the Cal South and the AYSO National Hall of Fame. He passed in 2007, but his impact is still felt to this day by those he touched, including me, because it was Norm who suggested that I get back into the game via coaching.

I began the licensing procedure with the United States Soccer Federation D License (it was a lot easier in those days) and enjoyed it so much that I flew through the different levels and ended up with my USSF A license in 1994, the year the US hosted the World Cup.

Once again I got to "live the dream" as I volunteered to be part of the organizing committee in Los Angeles. It was a great experience and fascinating to see the work it took to host the biggest event on the planet. That was also the first time I got to see Eric Wynalda, although our paths didn't cross physically.

I was lucky enough to work with some of the movers and shakers who eventually headed up Major League Soccer, including Ivan Gazidis, who is now the CEO at Arsenal. I also got an inside track on some choice tickets, including the historic USA versus Columbia match at the Rose Bowl and the final (or snooze fest depending on which way you looked at it) between Brazil and Italy. No need to say whom I was supporting!

With my licenses in hand and a few handy references from some big wigs, I began coaching club, high school, and college as well as a few amateur teams. In 1997, I rolled up to Windward High School, a small private school on the Westside of Los Angeles who were looking to build a program, and now 19 years later after eight league titles and one state championship, I'm very proud to still say I'm the Head Coach of the boys' program.

Over the years, I've taken more coaching courses, because you can't afford to stand still, including the National Soccer Coaches Association of America Premier Diploma, and I'm currently enrolled in the Master Coach and Soccer Leader course, which is an intense six-month program culminating at the 2017 NSCAA convention, which is located in Los Angeles.

So back to the top, I've decided to write a book about the trials and tribulations of coaching in club and high school soccer. This is without a doubt one of the fastest growing industries in the US, with millions of active players, coaches, administrators, and parents.

I've got 30 years of soccer coaching experience to share with you. Some of this information may seem obvious, some things you may already be doing (there's nothing like validation), but here and there I'm hopeful that there will be a golden nugget for you, a nugget that will make you look like the coaching genius we both know you are. I hope you enjoy!

Imposter Syndrome

I bet you're wondering why I'm beginning this book with a chapter on imposter syndrome. Well, the reason is that every now and again, we'll show up to practice or a game and be hit with a wave of dread. That moment when you think that you're a coaching fraud and everyone is about to find out that you haven't got a clue how to manage a group of young boys, girls, grown men, and women.

If you're a parent reading this book, you might wonder how the infamous "imposter syndrome" can strike on the sidelines. As your child gets deeper into the sport, you will likely encounter yourself, your child, or even their coaches facing imposter syndrome, so it's helpful to stick through this chapter so you can become aware of and spot the root causes and consequences of imposter syndrome… and what you can do about it.

I'm here to say that you're not crazy and you're not alone in feeling that you wished you had stayed in bed. You can and do overcome this feeling all the time, just like I managed to overcome my own imposter syndrome in the two main phases of my soccer career.

The first in TV, working for Fox Soccer Channel from 2000 to 2012, and the second when teaming up with former United States international, Eric Wynalda, and Cal FC, as we created history in the US Open Cup.

Taking on a leadership role along with mentoring is a huge responsibility that many people shy away from – you, on the other hand, have taken the chance to stand on that platform where everyone can see you. Doubt is a natural reaction, and even the best have their moments.

So here is a story you might enjoy. The year is 1999, and I've been dating a young woman who convinced me that I should go back to college and finish my degree. I fought this idea tooth and nail… I mean what 35-year-old wants to go and sit in a classroom with a bunch of 18 year-olds? After much nagging, I finally relented, signed up for a full load of classes (4) and immediately loved it. It was the best thing that ever happened to me, so thank you, Jackie!

One of the classes I enrolled in was broadcasting, where I met another young lady (hey, I can't help it if they love an English accent) named Dianna, who suggested I take my talents to Fox Sports West. She was convinced they'd give me an internship as I could commentate on two flies crawling across the classroom wall.

Uplifted by her enthusiasm, I went to Fox Sports West, a local sports channel in Century City. I met a producer, who when I said I wanted to intern looked at me like I had three eyes and two heads… "Thanks Nick, but aren't you a little old for interning? I mean most of the interns we get are barely out of diapers." I assured him that I was bang up for the role and he sent me off to an editing bay with a box full of tapes containing games from UCLA basketball.

After 60 minutes of logging jump shots, slam dunks, and a variety of other plays I realized that perhaps this interning lark wasn't actually for me. As I walked back to his office with the box of tapes ready to tell him that perhaps he was right, fate appeared and changed my life forever.

A young man named Choco was at an edit bay cutting up highlights of a Premier League match. I immediately hit the brakes, asked what he was doing and who he was working for. Unbeknownst to me, Fox Sports World was based two floors up from Fox West and shared the edit bays with Fox Sports West… boom!

I immediately dumped the basketball tapes back where they belonged, met the coordinator for Fox Sports World, and was interning that very weekend at 5 am PST logging English Premier League highlights and any other match they would give me.

Yes, I was the oldest person in the logging station by about 17 years and working for free, but I knew I'd found my place, my reason for being, and basically why I'd been put on this earth. I didn't miss a weekend for seven months, and at the end of the 1999/2000 season, I was offered a full-time job as a production assistant for the staggering amount of… $8 an hour, roughly $20K a year, plus benefits!

This required me giving up my budding career as a set-designer for movie junkets that paid $50 an hour. Hmmm… Russell Crowe or Alan Shearer…? I didn't give it a second's thought because I knew – and more importantly saw – the path and the potential pot of gold at the end of the rainbow.

The summer of 2000 was epic as the European Championships played out in Belgium/Holland and would eventually be won by that great French team when they beat Italy with David Trezeguet scoring **that** golden goal winner.

It was also the tournament that I began to write and voice teases and packages. These were the features that would air before the match or during half-time. Wow, I was in heaven and didn't think it could get much better, but more was to follow as the Premier League season began that August.

Instead of doing the PA grunt work of logging and editing, I began writing and voicing every Premier League tease… As you might remember, FSW used to show every match either live (well, sort of live) and on tape delay. That was 10 games a week!

Before you knew it, I was asked to start introducing the matches… LIVE! This was known as a wrap as you'd introduce the viewers to the stadium, whizz through the line-ups, and toss to the on-site announcer. As soon as the half-time whistle went, I'd jump back in and send to commercial break before coming back to voice the highlights and some promotions for upcoming games.

At the end of full-time, I'd then quickly wrap before sending back to break. Now I know this used to piss everyone off because viewers wanted to hear the match announcer and color commentator finish their thoughts and take in the ambience of the crowds, which sometimes was mental. The reason we had to do this was because of commercial time considerations and the two-hour window of the broadcasts. Sometimes the announcers would get super wordy, and the producers never wanted to cut them off in mid-flow as that sounded like crap, so rather than take a chance of going over the time slot, which on TV is worse than kissing your sister, I'd jump in to save those precious seconds. I hope all is forgiven now, but I agree I'd have much rather listened to the site announcers than the muppet in a voice-over booth in Los Angeles.

Anyway, back to the start of August 2000... gulp! Voicing teases to tape was fine as you could mess up repeatedly and trust me, I did, but LIVE... c'mon!

I had no experience and really no right to be behind a microphone. If I'm honest, I'd pretty much blagged (slang for wheedling) my way through things up until this point by just knowing more about soccer than everyone else, but I had zero TV experience. My saving grace was that the other Muppets – namely, Max Bretos, Christian Miles, and Allen Hopkins – barely had more TV experience than me, plus they hadn't followed the English Premier League, and to be fair the world game, quite as intently as I had.

I vividly remember being in the voice-over booth and the director/producer counting down from 10, 9, 8, 7, 6... to me being LIVE on air and introducing Manchester United versus Newcastle United from Old Trafford, opening day of the season!

Oh man, my fraud alert and imposter syndrome were going bananas. Somehow I managed to stumble through two minutes of airtime, mangling and inventing new words. I'm guessing we've all had that moment when two minutes actually felt like two hours...

it isn't pleasant. My mouth was dry, hands wet, and my butt cheeks ached from being so tightly clenched!

It took almost three months before that feeling finally started to dissipate. In those early days, I can honestly say there were games I dreaded introducing, as I knew the audience would be large and include many of my coaching friends, colleagues, and family.

The same thing happened all over again when I became the host of Fox Football Fone-In, first with Steven Cohen and then later with Eric Wynalda.

Now instead of it being a simple voice-over and knowing that I could hide behind images of the game, players, and stadium, it was me in the flesh and talking LIVE. Let me tell you... there were times when I thought I was going to pass out, the pressure was so intense and the fear of failure so great.

Who was I to be the voice of soccer? What had I done to earn this right? These were the type of questions that were banging around my head as the show went out LIVE to soccer fans across the country. I'm surprised I didn't have a sick bag underneath the desk, just in case.

Other than working hard and being in the right place at the right time, I didn't deserve this, shouted my imposter (and a couple of viewers who would email every week calling me a useless).

Two years later the imposter made a guest appearance as I managed to feel this way at the World Cup final in 2002 as well. My first major assignment as the chief soccer writer for foxsoccer.com saw me flying out to South Korea and Japan, all expenses paid, to cover 26 matches in 31 days!

I can clearly recall sitting in the press box at the Seoul World Cup Stadium for the opening match between the champions France against their former colony Senegal and thinking "what the hell are you doing here."

Can you imagine, just two years into the job and still technically classed as a PA, being the only US Fox representative at the World Cup Finals. I was pinching myself daily and not quite believing I was in the location where the entire soccer world wanted to be. I had had no official training as a journalist or writer, I just word-spewed on a laptop and hoped for the best. So thank you, Ed and Liam, the best editors ever.

For the 12 years I was at Fox, imposter syndrome would come and go however that wasn't the only place it would show up. It has also reared its ugly head to me as a soccer coach.

As I mentioned at the beginning of this book, I began coaching pretty much as soon as I arrived in the US back in 1987. I didn't really have a clue how to coach, but going in my favor was an accent and the ability to kick a ball better than most. I took the licenses mandated by the United States Soccer Federation, but if I'm honest I don't feel like they made me a better coach... however, they did make me a better BS artist as I could spout the current jargon of the time.

I coached various youth teams, some were better than others, but I still had moments where I thought I didn't belong... especially when my teams got crushed. That feeling intensified during my time coaching while I was at Fox because parents and players had heard and seen me on TV, pontificating about soccer as an expert!

Each loss was greeted with that painful silence, and the stares followed by whispering groups, with what I thought were discussions saying that it was my entire fault. Of course, this wasn't the case all the time, but in my mind, well, it was a tsunami of rubbish that was flowing my way.

After I left Fox in May of 2012, I got a phone call from Eric Wynalda asking for a favor. He was doing some UEFA Champions League stuff, and he couldn't make a training session for Cal FC, a team he'd formed with Mike Friedman. He asked if I could step in and coach the session for him. Of course, I agreed.

I drove out to the Glendale Soccer Complex in Los Angeles and had in mind a session I wanted to run. I also had no idea as to the quality and standard of players.

From the first moment of the warm-up, it was obvious that I was working with players of a caliber that I hadn't encountered before. Pablo Cruz, Jesus Gonzalez, Beto Navarro, Danny Barrera, Michael Randolph are all players who have played or eventually showed up in the NASL and MLS while Richie Menjivar and Derby Carrillo ended up representing their national team, El Salvador, in World Cup qualifiers!

Can anyone say "out of your league?"

Thankfully I had used one of my favorite resources, YouTube, before heading out to practice, and looked at a couple of high-level Ajax drills. Ajax are a Dutch club and were part of the "total football" revolution that took over soccer in the 1970s. The concept of their game at this particular time was that every player could interchange position and perform with a high degree of technical and tactical skill anywhere on the pitch.

The drill I decided to work these top players on was based mainly on the concept of one touch passing, receiving the ball with both the left and right foot, along with third man running (third man running is devastating because frequently the runner comes from the blind side of a two-man play and defenders, focused on the ball don't anticipate the run until it is too late). As they were going through this exercise, I felt like they knew I was a fraud, but because the drill was so demanding technically, and the fact that I noticed a couple of pertinent coaching points, I managed to pull it off.

Now don't get me wrong, they all turned their noses up at the fitness work I wanted them to do at the end of the session. I guess I had made an impression, though, because as I drove home, Wynalda called and said "you've got the job," to which I replied, "what job?" and he said "that was an audition to be the coach of the team while I'm away on UEFA Champions League duty for Fox in Germany."

And so with that call began a remarkable run with a team that would make history in the US Open Cup of 2012.

The Open Cup began in 1913 and is the oldest national soccer competition in the US. It is also the world's third longest running open soccer tournament. Who says the US doesn't have soccer history!

Like its name implies, it's open to anybody within the American soccer pyramid, from Major League Soccer to amateur teams in US club soccer, which is what Cal FC.

Cal FC had no home ground or fixed training venue, but somehow we qualified from the Southern California sectionals in Pamona and ended up facing the Kitsap Pumas in the 1st round proper of the competition.

The Pumas are based in Bremerton, Washington so early one morning in late May, the team met at Los Angeles International airport and flew to Seattle, followed by a very pleasant boat trip across the Puget Sound, and then two mini-busses to the hotel in preparation for the game.

Wynalda had left me one instruction, as is his way, before he left for Munich, and that was, "don't freakin' lose."

Before I'd really taken it all in, I was shaking hands with the opposing coach and handing the starting line-up to the referee. The technical area beckoned, and I was the boss for a proper match of soccer.

Holy crap, this is serious, and once again the imposter started tapping me on the shoulder. "Get out of the technical area,

Webster. Everyone knows you're a fraud. You'll be found out. You might talk a good game, but this is the real thing."

Oh boy, the noise in my head was nearly as loud as the crowd... And it was at that moment I changed. I looked at the players, and for some reason, I could tell that they trusted me to make the right decisions. I immediately became more comfortable and had what you'd call a moment of pure clarity by accepting the following facts about my imposter syndrome...

I had a pretty big part to play in my success. I had been feeling like a fraud because I was unable to internalize my success without voices jumping into my head. I thought I was given an opportunity that others weren't, so any achievement wasn't really deserved. When I managed to accept the fact that I'd put myself out there and learned that opportunities come to those who expose themselves to them, I started gaining some inner acceptance.

I needed to see coaching badges for what they are. They actually don't mean that much. The USSF, NSCAA, USYSA, or any other acronym in vogue, has decided that a particular country's style is the standard way to teach the sport. They usually go all in for whatever happens to be in fashion, so currently Germany and France are all the rage, however, four years from now it could be Argentina and Holland, we just never know.

Don't measure yourself by credentials and coaching badges, however, *do* attend courses and conventions. It's at these events that you'll find validation if you're doing things right and you might make a few connections that can last a lifetime.

Realize that when you hold back, you're robbing your players. If you show up to practice or games and you're feeling like you don't deserve to be there, I can guarantee those vibes are going to rub off on some of your players who just might also be suffering from imposter syndrome. Remember that almost everyone – including Eric Wynalda – has doubts!

During my time at Fox Soccer Channel I had the chance to ask deep, thoughtful questions to some of the biggest names in the sport and every so often you'd see doubt creep into the eyes of players and managers about what they thought was the correct answer.

Say what you can. As the coach you're considered the expert, the Oracle, the Yoda in a tracksuit! All of the supporters if you're standing in the technical area of the stadium, and all of the parents if you're coaching youth soccer, think that you know everything there is to know about the game… and well, you can't know everything. Just be honest and say what you know and if you don't know the answer, give it the old classic "let me get back to you on that'"… you'll still be respected.

I used these same principles at Fox and added the following…

I started to focus on the value I was providing. Not to disparage my American colleagues, but the viewers at home said they found that an English voice introducing the English Premier League just sounded more authentic. That didn't stop me from thinking about what they thought of me, but I felt less of a fraud because I felt like I knew what I was talking about and was giving good information.

I kept all the emails, good and bad. Let me tell you something… the first time you get hate mail, it cuts deeper than any knife, sharp or blunt. You think that your career is over because you know that your boss has read them as well, however on the other side of the coin there was nothing quite like getting some fan email. There is a yin and yang of being out there as a personality, so anytime the imposter would come sneaking around, I'd go back into the archives and pull out a "Webster, you're great!" email.

And perhaps most importantly, I learned to recognize imposter syndrome when it started tapping my shoulder. I learned over time to do the following…

Say "It's Imposter Syndrome, " and it immediately becomes less important and terrible. It made it easier to confront what was happening head on.

So back to the 1ˢᵗ round of the US Open Cup and the Pumas who were then-USL PDL champions. The match started at a fast pace, the Ajax concepts I had shown the players started flowing, and three hours later we were all at the 19ᵗʰ Hole Bar & Grill, Bremerton.

Yep, the entire squad just letting loose after deservedly getting the win that was to start a journey which none of us knew where we'd end up.

I wouldn't recommend this approach as part of your teams' recovery process, and in all fairness, this isn't how professionals treat their bodies, but this was a one-off and richly deserved because it was so unexpected.

The amount of sunglasses being worn that morning as we made our way back to Seattle/Tacoma airport at 7 am told the story of Cal FC. However, we were in the 2nd round and drawn to face the Wilmington Hammerheads of the USL… in North Carolina, six days later!

On Friday we had a training session in Glendale and the vibe, as Mike Friedman loved to say, was happening. Training was up-tempo and the competition fierce as everyone wanted to make the trip to North Carolina, but only 18 would be allowed to travel. With Eric still in Germany, I was his eyes and ears.

There is nothing like proper competition to make practices hum, and I can't wait for the day when you all have the opportunity to work with a big talented squad when only 11 starting spots are on the line.

On Sunday we began the journey to Wilmington NC for a Tuesday game and let me tell you this, US soccer didn't make it easy!

To enable amateur teams to participate, US Soccer helps with the travel expenditure by giving the team a budget. There is a catch, though, and that is you have to use US Soccer's travel agent, and with no direct flights to Wilmington it was going to be a long day for everyone.

We couldn't travel as a team, and everyone had multiple stops to get to Wilmington, in some cases taking 10 hours and three flights... nice preparation, eh?

I arrived late Sunday night and scoped out a nice patch of beach for us to train on Tuesday morning before the game. We also had one session at Legion Stadium on Monday evening to get a taste of the turf field, which was like walking on the surface of the sun. The temperature was in the high 90s with humidity to match, a massive difference from Los Angeles and Bremerton.

Eric finally arrived from Munich late Tuesday afternoon, and we headed off to the stadium to take on a very good Hammerheads team who were looking to make their own run in the Cup. The reward for the winners would be a trip to Portland to face off against the MLS Portland Timbers at their atmospheric stadium, Providence Park (then called Jeld-Wen Field).

The cramped away dressing room reminded me of a broom closet, and due to the humidity it was also like a sauna, however, the banter in the dressing room was outstanding, and the players were really up for it.

With a decent crowd on hand both Eric and I thought it would be a tough game and one we'd be lucky to win.

What did we know?

We battered the professional team 4-0, and it was never even close. The players had so much belief, and their mindset that I've discussed earlier in the book was outstanding. There was never a doubt in their heads that they wouldn't win and it all stemmed from beating the Kitsap Pumas.

Somehow that victory and the celebration afterward had flicked a switch in their mentality. Yes, they were all accomplished players, but until that point they'd all been "yer but" players.

"Yer but" was a term Eric used to describe players who had the ability and should've been playing or at least competing for a spot in the MLS but when talked about by other coaches the conversation would go like this. "Don't you think so and so is a good player – yer but, let me tell you about this flaw."

Now they were anything but "yer but" players and the celebration, while raucous in the small dressing room, was much more muted in the nearby restaurant we retired to. In fact, everyone was back in bed before midnight. We all had multiple early morning flights back to Los Angeles and only six days to prepare for MLS big boys, the Portland Timbers.

We met up again as a team on the Saturday at a local high school in Los Angeles for a training session that was more like a media session. Fox Soccer and other local media outlets were interested in this story.

A team coached by Eric Wynalda and his former Fox Football Fone-In partner, Nick Webster, were now making some noise. Interviews, photos, and autographs were now the name of the game as history beckoned.

Once again, US Soccer, who some would say had a grudge against Eric for his outspoken comments about the national team, MLS, and in fact, anything to do with American soccer, had us fly through San Jose to get to Portland. I mean, really, are there no direct flights from LAX to Portland?

We left LAX on Tuesday morning, arriving in Portland mid-afternoon, and did the customary mini-bus convoy to the hotel in downtown Portland. After dropping off our packs, we headed straight to Jeld-Wen Field to get the flight out of our legs.

The session was garbage though as the majority of the players looked like they'd all taken a sleeping pill or something. It was obvious that the magnitude of what we were trying to achieve had begun to kick in, or maybe the players knew something I didn't. After all, no amateur team had ever beaten an MLS team – except on penalties – in the US Open Cup before.

We'd also heard that the Timbers, who hadn't played the previous weekend, were going to field their strongest eleven. This eleven contained six international players. The task ahead seemed like Mt. Everest to our merry band of misfits.

In the early evening, I took the Barrera brothers (Danny and Diego) and Derby Carrillo (my roommate) out for a game of disc golf. This was becoming part of our ritual before matches and another indicator to me that I was an accepted and respected part of the team. By the way, Danny and Diego are excellent at disc golf, so don't get sandbagged by them as Derby and myself spent more time climbing trees looking for our discs than throwing them while getting relieved of a few dollars in the process.

That night, Fox showed up with Mark Rogondino to do a ton of interviews for TV as the media machine started kicking into overdrive. Eric and the players took their turns in front of the camera.

After Mark and the cameras left we had a quick team meeting, and it was really cool when the players owned up to having a garbage training session because I thought it might have been my fault (imposter syndrome). The fact that they took accountability was not lost on Eric, who was quick to point out that players love making excuses for not performing. He believed that with the ownership and accountability the players were taking, we had a chance no matter what line-up John Spencer, the Timbers coach, sent out the following evening.

Wednesday was game day, so I organized a walk around the park with some light stretching in the morning and subway sandwiches for lunch, big time, eh!

Following an afternoon siesta, we met down in the lobby and Eric ordered a couple of Godfather cocktails for each of us. Whisky, Amaretto, on the rocks, in an old fashioned glass. I knew that despite his cocky exterior, he must be nervous!

The drive to the stadium took us through downtown Portland and past bars where fans were getting their pre-match lubrication going. The Open Cup might not be as big as the MLS Cup, but the Timber Army was taking it seriously, and a crowd of between 5,000-8,000 was expected.

In my Fox career, I've been to all the great temples of the beautiful game. Wembley, the Nou Camp, Old Trafford, the Westfalen, you name it, I've been to these amazing stadiums… but I'd never been as someone who was about to compete mentally and physically.

The dressing room at Jeld-Wen Field wasn't like Wilmington - this was a palace. Players got ready and had room to knock the ball back and forth. Eric paced the floor, and I did what I'd done for weeks, which was tell the players how great they are… yes, players – regardless of how good they are – still feel insecure and need an arm around the shoulder now and again.

The feeling of pride and sense of achievement as I took the bench with the players and Eric for this 3rd round tie between David and Goliath was a sensational moment.

The first half was a blur of Timber chances as their teamwork and fitness levels kept Cal FC firmly on the back foot. Our dressing room at half-time looked like a battlefield of broken bodies as the players literally collapsed on the floor. However, it was still 0-0, and we were still in the game.

Eric didn't address the team until the last minute, yet he spoke quietly to every player, reminding them of the opportunity they had worked for. That approach made a powerful impression on me and is one I've used during my coaching career in stressful and pressurized moments.

The second half was a repeat of the first, but still, the Timbers couldn't finish, despite creating quality opportunities. Derby

Carrillo, kept on finding himself perfectly positioned in goal and really wasn't forced into outstanding saves, instead making routine saves.

At the other end of the pitch we weren't creating anything noteworthy but did manage to carve out some quality moments of possession. Then in the 79th minute, Richie Menjivar was called for a handball in the box as he lifted his arms to block a cross. Kris Boyd, Portland's high-priced designated player, stepped up for the penalty that would surely end our dreams… and smacked it over the bar!

Talk about getting out of jail… Derby had already committed to his dive, and Boyd could have passed the ball into the back of the net, but on this night the footballing gods were smiling on little Cal FC.

At the end of full-time, all of our players were physically and mentally spent, but the adrenalin Wynalda created in the huddle just before extra-time began will always live in my memory. He talked about love, relationships, and the one moment that could change the players' lives forever.

Sure enough, five minutes into extra-time, Danny Barrera crafted a pass from nothing and Artur Aghasyan timed his run, outsprinted the Portland back line, and cheekily dinked the goalkeeper, 1-0.

Barrera ran to me, and I don't think I've ever hugged anybody that hard. Wynalda was pointing and shouting at everyone to keep concentrating, which you can imagine, was quite hard to do when all of a sudden you actually start thinking about winning a game that 100 minutes earlier was nothing more than fantasy.

The old adage about being most vulnerable when you've just scored is so true as we almost conceded immediately, however, there was such desperation in the Timbers' play that they kept snatching at their chances.

Seconds started taking minutes, while minutes felt like hours. Those were the longest 25 minutes I've ever experienced in a soccer match but somehow we held on to win 1-0 and became the first amateur team to score and beat an MLS team without the aid of a penalty shoot-out. We had created history!

The Timbers Army gave us an amazing reception after giving their team plenty of stick, chanting "Beat Seattle," as they would be our next opponents.

The post-game celebrations in the dressing room were great as the last fumes were expended in joy and then everyone hit empty. No one, including Eric or myself, had anything left in the tank. I remember going out for a beer, but nobody had anything to say, we'd just look at each other, laugh, and basically shut down, spent in every conceivable way.

If you have a couple of hours free and want to see how the giant was slayed, there is a link to the entire game, including post-game reaction from Spencer and Wynalda on YouTube.

Heading back to Los Angeles the following morning – via San Jose, of course (thanks, US Soccer) – I had the opportunity to reflect on what I had achieved. I'd banished "imposter syndrome" and knew that no matter what anybody said, I had played a significant part in a truly historic event.

My relationships with the players were so important to our success and even though I had a ton of soccer knowledge that wasn't the important part. It was about love, respect, egos, and management, all qualities that don't require a coaching badge but do require listening, watching, and knowing when to step in and perhaps most importantly, when to get out of the way.

The following week was a blur as we began our preparations to play the three-time defending US Open Cup champions, the Seattle Sounders. The game would be nationally televised on Fox Soccer Channel, who had mysteriously become our shirt sponsor. I say mysteriously because no one ever saw any money from that deal...!

Once again, US Soccer made our travel arrangements tricky as we had to repeat our performance of flying through San Jose. We also missed out on playing at Qwest Field (capacity 69,000) because of an Open Cup deal the Sounders had made with Starfire Stadium (capacity 4,500), which was a shame.

The vibe around the team was changing ever so slightly as well. With the game being televised, players knew this was their chance to get in the shop window. Agents started appearing out of nowhere, and the focus shifted from we to I.

I'm certainly not saying that was the cause of the stuffing we received from the Sounders as Sigi Schmid fielded a team that contained 10 internationals and were coming off a 9-day break.

Just to offer a contrast, we had been on the road since May 15th, and in the to and fro travelled 2,354 miles to Bremerton, Washington; 5,296 to Wilmington, North Carolina; 2,014 to Portland, Oregon; and 2,358 back to the Pacific Northwest and Seattle for a grand total of 12,002 miles in 20 days.

I'm very proud that we managed to hold off the Sounders until the 50th minute, but as soon as they scored, I knew we were cooked. I said to Eric, "They'll hit us for six..." They ended up getting five!

It was a sad dressing room at the end of the match as we all knew that we'd be scattering around the country. The run and that dream was over, but for many of the players better dreams were about to begin.

Derby Carrillo is still playing professionally in El Salvador and has represented his country 13 times.

Danny Barrera is currently the captain of Sacramento Republic FC.

Beto Navarro went to Atlanta and now plays with Jacksonville Armada in the NASL.

Richie Menjivar has played for his national team 31 times and represents Rayo OKC.

Eder Arreola is playing for FC Shirak in Armenia.

Eric returned to Fox, while briefly having a spell with the Atlanta Silverbacks, who he managed to the 6th round of the Open Cup in 2014. More of that later, though, as I was alongside him for a 5th round match vs. the Colorado Rapids that featured seven ejections and me coaching the Silverbacks for the last 40 minutes!

This chapter was dedicated to "imposter syndrome" and a little of my coaching and broadcasting career. The imposter still peeks its head around the corner from time to time but using some of the tips to spot him, I can tell him where to go. So anytime you find yourself in a position where you're wondering if you belong on the stage, steady yourself, and know that you're not alone – I'm with you!

Creating Culture in a Soccer Club/Team

If ever a team sport was designed with culture in mind, soccer is surely that sport, because although the coach is the spiritual leader, it is at the end of the day a player's game. Once players cross that white line they're basically at liberty to do what they want within the laws of the game, and as a coach you can only affect that by either taking them out of the game via substitution or waiting for half-time.

Time and energy must be poured into the creation of culture, and let me tell you from experience, a trip to the dentist for a root canal can be more appealing in some circumstances.

Let's start with this question... have you ever been on a team with that losing, down-in-the-dump vibe, the team heaving with negativity, poor attitudes, unhealthy jealousy, and just oozing conflict? It's not a great place to be, it's not a great place to practice or play, and as for performing your best, that's a pipe dream.

So just what is culture? It's a difficult thing to pinpoint and means different things to different people. In my book, culture consists of values, attitudes, and beliefs relating to the sport of soccer.

To develop the right culture, the team and/or coach has to figure out where they want to go as a team. Is the focus of the team on fun, mastery, or training players for the next level... or flat out winning?

Once we have identified what the shared mission is we can then formulate the culture from this starting place. For example, it's useless having a culture of fun if most of the squad are tearing each other's throats out in practice because they're so determined to win.

The culture creates norms of behavior on a team and members learn exactly what is and what isn't allowed.

These norms establish guidelines on how to communicate with each other, work together, and most importantly in a physical team sport like soccer, how to deal with conflict.

When everyone knows what the culture is, everyone in theory will be more likely to follow the herd than branch out on their own. This allows the culture to develop an atmosphere within the team that guides its experiences.

When a team has a defined culture that is understood by all of its members, they feel an implicit pressure (in the good sense) to support that culture.

Let's start with the building blocks of culture ...

- COMMITMENT (to a higher cause, purpose, each other)
- RESPONSIBILITY (accept your role)
- ACCOUNTABILITY (give and take critique)
- INTEGRITY (gap between what you say and what you do)
- RESPECT (for the game, opponent, self, coach, team, and referee)
- TRUST (yourself, others, coach)
- LEADERSHIP (this is everyone's work)
- COURAGE/COMPASSION - (give)
- SERVICE (sacrifice/suffering)
- HUMILITY (others get credit, gratitude, and

thankfulness)

When you sit down with your team ask the following questions:

- What values do we want to act as the foundation for our team culture?
- What attitudes and beliefs about your sport, competition, and team do you want to hold?
- What are the goals that the team wants to pursue?
- How do the athletes and coaches want to treat each other?
- What kind of atmosphere do we want on our team?

When you ask and answer these questions, you are proactively developing a team culture of your team's own design rather than leaving it to chance. In doing so, you are building a team that has its best chance of being positive and supportive and, as a result, performing at its highest level possible.

Learn from the Past

We all have experiences from which we can draw valuable lessons. If you're a first-time coach, examine the cultures of teams you played for previously. What worked for you in those cultures? What didn't? Similarly, if you're a seasoned coach, think about the cultures you created in the past. What cultivated success?

Create a Culture that Aligns with Your Core Values

This is your club/team. You're driving it, and you need to infuse who you are into what you do. Otherwise, it won't work. Think about your personality and, more importantly, your core values. Are you ingeniously innovative or unwittingly creative? Do you foster a "work hard, play hard" mentality? Are you relaxed but also expect the best from people? If so, create that balance of work and play. Are you a true collaborator? Then advance that behavior in your club and reward the people who embrace it. Take time to reflect on who you are, the vibe you want to radiate, and, ultimately, the kind of culture that fits both you and your club

Find Great People Who Complement You

Round out your club culture by hiring people who offer different experiences than yours. As tempting as it may be, avoid hiring a "mini-me." Identify your strengths and weaknesses, then fill in the gaps.

For example, if you are an amazing tactical coach but fall short when it comes to talking to administrators and parents, bring in a savvy director who likes talking in public. If you are an all-out attacking coach, hire someone who is more conservative and specializes in defending. Diverse perspectives grounded in a shared vision are worth their weight in gold. Again, just be sure not to sacrifice your core values.

Communicate

When developing culture, talk with each other. This might sound trite, but it's easier said than done. People need to be able to share their ideas and speak openly without fear of repercussion. People want their opinions heard, and they want to feel good.

This millennial generation needs to hear their voices – it's just the way it is.

Have Fun

It's simple: a little fun goes a long way. Granted, this looks different for every club/team. There are ways to engage players in activities that feel less like work. For example, declare shoot-out Fridays during the hard parts of the season where the legs and minds are heavy. Take your team bowling, go to a McDonald's, or hold a contest. Just do something out of context and give players the freedom to relax, show up in a different way and have fun.

Invite People to Drink the Kool-Aid

Bottom line, every one needs to be a believer. If you don't stand for anything, you stand for nothing.

Work as a Team

Stop thinking of people in terms of "squad members" or "defenders/attackers." You're all part of the same team, so act like it. Rallying around the idea "we're all in this together" builds a sense of unity and community, which fosters culture.

The best people are team players who truly support the team, its founders, its administrators, and their teammates.

Maintain and Carefully Evolve Your Culture

Culture is not something you put in place and expect it to stay forever. It takes work. You need to nurture it. You also need to give it the freedom to evolve. If you cling too tightly to your culture, you risk smothering it. Protect it, yes, but understand that your culture will shrink and swell – and that's okay as long as it maintains its core.

Effectively evolving your club/team culture sometimes requires making hard decisions to let go of people who don't evolve with it.

DEALING WITH PARENTS & CRITICISM

Doesn't it drive you crazy when a parent rolls up to you and starts telling you that you don't know your butt from your head? "Coach, my son has so much pace, he's a great defender, he's got a big boot, my daughter is a special player, she scored 10 goals in one game... blah, blah, blah."

Unfortunately, it happens all the time because parents cannot see further than their own child. How do I know this, you may ask... well, I've got my own budding Lionel Messi, who quite frankly is already the best nine-year-old soccer player to have ever graced planet earth!

No, seriously, he's that good. You should see him skin the Orange Crush U8's. He scores five goals a game, takes awesome throw-ins, goal kicks, free kicks, penalties, and did I mention the five assists and...

I would like to think that I've got a handle on what he can and can't do, however on every team, there is at least one, possibly two, and if you're really unlucky four or five complete "nutters" who really do believe that their child is the second coming. How do they know? Well, they just know, because "you don't know him/her like we do" – it's a classic situation and one that will drive you from the team and the sport if you're not careful.

The key to surviving this is boundaries and the subtle art of deflecting.

Living in Southern California I've had them all, including some staggeringly rich parents who think that they can buy you, ones that love you to pieces, then plunge the knife deeper than you can possibly imagine, and complete loonies that hated me from the off. I remember once being in a boardroom on the top floor of the swankiest offices in Century City as two sets of parents fought over the right to sack or keep me (I got sacked!!!)... and, they'd both hired expensive lawyers to win their argument! You name it, I've probably dealt with it.

So here is my advice to you when dealing with parents...

Have a pre-season meeting before the first practice to discuss your plans and expectations for the season. Don't, whatever you do, say you're going to win the league, state, tournaments, etc. That is like committing professional suicide because if you don't deliver where can you go from there? However, encourage lots of questions from the parents and let them know that you have given a lot of thought to how you're going to coach their children. Definitely use the phrase "what questions do you have?" and put the onus on them.

Always express appreciation for their interests and concerns. This will make them more open and at ease with you. Definitely use the responses, "I understand where you're coming from" and "I feel your concerns" and look them in the eye when you're doing this and not your cell phone.

Always listen to their ideas and feelings, no matter how outlandish they are, and try your best not to interrupt when they're going on a ramble about how their kid has always played midfield and now they're having a tough time playing right back (especially if the child is six years old!).

Remember, they are interested and concerned because it is their child however, I draw the line when talking about another parent's child. I always say "I'll talk to you about your child for hours, but I'll never speak about someone else's kid." It's not professional and can lead to some epic problems, even if you know the child they want to talk about is a problem.

Know what your objectives are and do what you believe to be of value to the team, not to the parents. No coach can please everyone, and if you try to go down that route, you'll ultimately fail and make yourself miserable in the process.

Know your club/high school rules and policies, along with the rules of the game. Be prepared to stand by them and to explain them in detail to parents because they do not always know the rules of the game and most certainly, haven't read the small print of a club or high school document.

Handle any confrontation one-on-one and not in a crowded situation. Try not to be defensive. Often parents just want to blow off some steam just by talking.

Yep, I know you're not paid nearly enough to be the team/parent shrink, but that's part of the job. If you listen to their point of view and then thank them, they'll think you're a genius.

Don't succumb to pressure, whether physical, mental, or material. You're the boss, and you get to make the final decision. This doesn't mean that you can't listen to parents, though. If advice is good, it's good. We just have to be big enough to accept good advice, turn around, and then use it!

Never let parents criticize their children in front of anyone else. Never let your players be humiliated by anyone, even by their own parents. Children look up to adults and if certain behaviors are allowed, then they will do the exact same thing when they are adults

Don't blame the players for their parents' actions. I know it's tempting to take a player out or even sit them on the bench because their parents are behaving out of line, but you can't take it out on the kids.

Be consistent! If you change a rule or philosophy during the season, you may be in for trouble. At the very least, inform players and parents of any change as soon as possible. And whatever you do, don't bend the rules for star players, it'll be the end of you.

Most importantly, be fair! If you treat all of your players fairly, you will gain their respect along with the goodwill of their parents. Yep, I know life isn't fair, especially when it comes to soccer. Blind referees, unruly parents, poorly behaved opponents and supporting the England national team, but nobody said it was fair.

The challenge and opportunity for you as a coach is to address these issues in a positive and forthright manner so that the season will be enjoyable for everyone involved. I've had "those other seasons, " and they are a nightmare that stay with you long even after that season has ended.

Now let's remember that not all parents are the same, and we have different kinds of egos and characters who want different things for their kids. To lump them all together would be a big mistake.

Dealing with "overly-helpful" parents is a classic scenario because you don't want to blow them off, but invariably they're the parents of your worst player!

If parents have been acting as your assistants at practices, it is not such a stretch of the imagination for them to want to continue to offer their two cents during games. This is something, which you need to watch closely, for several reasons.

If other parents see a "non-coach" (parent) giving instructions to players on the field, they are going to be tempted to start yelling out their own instructions. This will drive the kids crazy, because as the saying goes, "too many cooks" really do spoil things.

Most parents are going to be watching their own child – and giving most of their instructions to their own child, whether they plan to or not… it's just parental nature. I learned the hard way with my own boy, who after scoring a hat-trick in his first game (leading me to believe that I'd created the next Cristiano Ronaldo) then refused to listen to anything I had to say for the following twelve matches.

When they do call out another child's name, that's when the aggravation kicks up a notch.

Yelling out to kids can be very distracting (even when the instructions are good) because it takes attention away from the game and keeps them from using their own brains to figure things out.

Soccer is a game where the player's brain is a super computer that must make multiple decisions in the time it takes to blink an eye. Whatever you do, don't put bugs into that PC, because it will crash!

Furthermore, many children simply want praise and positive reinforcement from their parents – so any corrections/instructions have the potential to be viewed as a public statement of "you're not good enough" and "what are you doing?" Finally, and often most importantly, the instructions being given by these "experts" often tends to be completely wrong – and the polar opposite of what you have been working on at practice.

So now that I've given you some classic scenarios, what should you do?

The key is tact, patience, and the old velvet glove treatment – plus the preseason meeting we spoke about earlier. Explain to the parents that the kids need to be able to use the games as building blocks and learning experiences – too much criticism is going to give them the impression and feeling that the parents view them as failures.

Don't be a complete monster, but seriously enforce the rules to the parents that on game day the ONLY thing that you want to hear is praise "well done" and "do that again."

Tell your parent assistants that you really appreciate their help, but you need them to sit with the other parents on game day because you are concerned that other parents will be tempted to start "helping" by shouting instructions.

If you have some parent, who starts to give instructions, stamp this out immediately, no matter how uncomfortable it makes you feel. Each time a parent breaks this rule, smile, give them a look and politely remind them about the rule we've ALL AGREED upon regarding coaching from the sidelines.

At some pitches I've been to I've actually seen signs that say that this is a NO COACHING ZONE for parents, and while a little over the top, I can't say that I completely disagree with the sentiment. If parents can't stop yelling, you'll have to ask them to leave or even take the massive step of removing their child from the team.

The same goes for parents who want to yell at opposing players or referees. This behavior is completely unacceptable, and YOU as the spiritual leader of the team must make it crystal clear that this kind of conduct just doesn't happen on your watch. It is truly terrifying for younger players (U4 – U10) to deal with irate adults – and you need to stop this immediately.

If the parent can't listen and leave the playing area, don't be afraid to abandon/call off the game. Better yet, get someone in an official capacity if anyone is available to help. Remember, it is your JOB to protect all children – just as you would want the other coach to protect your players no matter how intimidating the behavior is.

I've experienced a parent when I coached in Florida who wanted to have a fistfight because I took his daughter out after she was reduced to tears by his screaming at her. It is a bananas situation that has the potential to escalate way quicker than you imagine. I took the high road in that situation and ran to my car quicker than Usain Bolt!

Dealing with parental complaints is an occupational hazard that we all have to eventually face up to. Almost every parent, whether they love or hate you, will at some point disagree with your decisions. The parent is simply putting their interests first, and as a parent myself, I can't completely fault them. And what you'll eventually discover is that most parents who constantly complain usually just move clubs and start the process of moaning again.

I really try and encourage professional and personal feedback through the use of forms, which while lacking in the personal touch are easy to put together online and can be as simple as 1) What did you like? and 2) What didn't you like? (even if it can be painful to read).

I would say that most parental feedback is well-intentioned and the parent simply wants an explanation for what is happening because they or their child do not understand your decision-making process. This feedback or questioning usually concerns playing time or positioning.

Look, most parents have two objectives when they sign their child up to participate in anything: 1) for their child to succeed and 2) for their child to be happy (just watch out for the parent who speaks first and foremost about winning).

If you praise the child in front of the parent, you're well on your way to achieving those two points – and you earn credit in both columns. Do this as often as you can without coming across as a complete brown noser, and this should most of the time keep complaints down to a minimum.

Anytime that you start resenting the time that it takes to give this positive feedback, tell yourself that you could easily be spending double the amount talking to just one upset parent!

In short, a good coach makes the parents believe that they have wonderful, successful, and happy offspring – which causes the parents to believe that the coach must be an absolutely brilliant judge of children.

But, of course, you cannot please all of the people all of the time – and on any team, I've ever coached there is always at least one complainer or advice-giver.

If this happens, listen briefly to find out what the problem is, then schedule a time to talk about it. NEVER discuss any serious problem right before a practice or right before a game. This is when you need to be laser focused on your players, your team, and your opponents. You don't need the distractions or aggravation and certainly don't need to be upset yourself if things get out of hand, which can happen when someone is popping off at you.

Furthermore, if the parent is really upset, you don't want any confrontation to occur in front of your players or other parents. So, set the discussion for another time not surrounding the team. NEVER discuss any problems or complaints right after a game. If a parent comes to you with a complaint right after a game, make up any excuse that you can and get out of there.

The 24-hour rule, which many teams employ, is absolutely vital for these situations, and one that I state at the first meeting I have with parents.

Usually, these complaints come after a tough loss, when everyone is upset because the beauty of soccer is that it's such an emotional game.

The 24-hour rule gives everyone time to cool off – so that things are not said which are regretted later.

So… it's now 24 hours later and either you call the parent, or they call you.

When you speak with the parent, listen carefully to what their perceived problem is. Let them talk… do not interrupt, no matter how tempting it is to defend your position. Be calm. Explain to them how you see things. Remember, lavish some praise on their child during the meeting (remember parental objectives). Try to verify their reports that the child is unhappy and the possible reasons why. Volunteer to have a meeting with them and the child to talk about the situation and talk about why you think what you're doing is best for the player. Usually, you will be able to resolve complaints by open communication, and a calm approach to the problem.

Obviously, not all parents will be satisfied, no matter what you do. Some parents, who were once decent athletes and then end up with non-athletic children, have a very hard time facing reality about their child's lack of talent.

If it is clear that you are not getting anywhere, suggest that you set up a joint meeting with club officials, the Technical Director, and/or the Athletic Directors to talk about the problem. In the meantime, call the administrative parties to give a "heads-up" a phone call is coming their way if it appears that the parent is truly irate.

If worse comes to worst, take heart that "parents-from-hell" tend to stick around for only a short time. Usually, you will find that they have been unhappy with every coach whom their child has ever had. At the end of the season they'll head back into the club pool and look for a new team.

BE ORGANIZED

If only the game were about balls, bibs, and cones, we'd all just stroll down onto the pitch, roll out the balls and tell our players to have at it. Sort of like how it was in the old days before coaches and parents came along and interfered with everything, because back in the "good old days" we just played.

Unfortunately, the "good old days" no longer exist. The street soccer of yesteryear is nothing but a black and white memory for many of us... while to the new generation, they can't fathom that we ever played in the streets.

Long gone are the days when my mom would stuff some breakfast down my neck, knowing full well I wouldn't eat anything all day before I rushed out the door to hang with my mates and play until she'd call me back for dinner ten hours later.

Those games were epic and would range from me kicking the ball alone against a wall with a crude goal sketched out in whatever paint, chalk, or mud I could find to mammoth 20 vs. 20 all-out wars. No coaches, no coaching, and no worries about being whisked off the street by some weirdo... ah, "the good old days."

Here in the 21st century, we're all a little paranoid (including myself – my little boy is 9 years old), and the thought of letting our kids wander down to the local park on their own is enough to get you locked up by the local authorities and shouted at by your wife or better half.

So how do we recreate the freedom of yesteryear for our players where success and failure don't matter because it's all about having fun?

This is the question that many coaches have been asking themselves for pretty much the last two decades, because ultimately, we want our players to have imagination and to be able to play without instruction.

This is where being organized comes into play. Now I know organization seems like a very simple thing to achieve and to be totally honest, it is, and yet it's something that coaches mess up all the time.

So below is my list to keep yourself organized. If you adhere to most of the components you'll have happy players... and more importantly, happy parents and administrators.

Be Early for Everything

Nothing will create more problems for you than showing up on time or late, regardless of the situation. There are always early birds who are super keen and can't wait to get practicing. The cool thing about the early birds is you can use them as assistants to help you set up.

Trust me when I tell you that nothing dazzles parents, athletic directors, and administrators more than for them to arrive at your practice field and see a field of cones, bibs, and balls laid out in pretty patterns. Yep, it doesn't matter if you haven't got a clue what you're going to do in the session... cones, bibs, and balls displayed in symmetrical patterns signify that you are in charge and that you are organized.

By arriving early, you also take out the stress of rushing and trying to corral players, who – depending on their age – once they arrive are similar to cats. Once you're setup, you can also pass, juggle, and chat with your players in a nice, relaxed way, which once again puts smiles on the faces of the people who matter, namely, the parents.

The same is true for matches and tournaments. I know it can be a royal pain in the butt, especially when you have to travel miles. You've looked that the match-ups, you're going to be there all day, and you know your team is going to get crushed but you're still the leader and you need to be in charge.

The perception that you're organized and on top of everything is the lasting impression you'll leave everyone.

When I was a younger coach and left things to chance, I can't tell you the grief I created for myself by not having cones and bibs on hand, and being on time.

Equipment

I've mentioned cones, and at less than 50 cents a pop, there really is no excuse for not having a nice stack of different colored cones. Remember, perception is a reality for many people. I have a mate, who to be fair is a good coach, however, I can't help but take the piss out of him because when you show up to some of his sessions, there is a visual feast of colored cones placed beautifully around the pitch. At the end of the day if you get to be known as the "Picasso of the Cones" it's not the worst coaching nickname to have in youth soccer.

Bibs, while more expensive than cones, are important as it gives you the ability to pick distinct teams and groups There's nothing worse than twelve players all wearing gray, and you want to work on a little six vs. six. Confusion will hit your players like a ton of bricks, and then, of course, the pesky parents will be whispering from the sidelines "the kids don't know what team they're on," "coach doesn't seem very organized today," among other things.

Bibs can also make great markers for laying out formations, plus you can use them as a training device, such as tails for your younger players when playing agility and running games.

I should also talk about portable goals… and now we get into the expenses surrounding what is the cheapest game to play. I use the fold-up Pugg goals, which can retail up to $120 a pair. Trust me, they are worth the expense because nothing beats the feeling of seeing and kicking a ball into the back of the net. Of course, you can make cone and bib goals, but the visceral experience of the ball hitting the back of the net is gone, plus you invariably end up with arguments as to whether the ball went over the cone/bib and therefore should not count as a goal.

One type of goal I would avoid like the plague is the plastic PVC variety. These are truly crap and usually break if you happen to glance in their direction, plus they're a pain in the butt to put together and then break down every practice.

If you have a budget to blow, I like the bownet goals, as they are the next best things, in my opinion, to full-size goals. They're super portable and allow players to really smash the ball into the back of the net. At close to $300 each, though, you're looking at a tidy outlay of close to $600 for a pair.

By now you may have noticed that I've not mentioned the most important piece of equipment in soccer, and without it, we don't have a game... namely, the ball.

My advice to you, and please take this to heart, is DON'T BUY ANY!!!

Yes, I am shouting because I can't tell you how many balls my players have lost over thirty years, but believe me when I say it runs into thousands of dollars.

Even before you hold your first practice make it known that you do not supply balls for practice. Sure, I may have a ball of my own that I'll use for demonstration purposes, but chances are that'll go missing the first time you turn your back.

My thinking here is this... if you are a soccer player, you must have your own ball. It's really very simple because you can't play soccer if you don't have a ball.

By making your players responsible for their own ball, you create the following scenarios for yourself...

You take away an unnecessary expense from yourself because even a cheap ball can run at $15+ or more.

You create a lot more room in the trunk/and or back seat of your car.

You get to remove the smell of wet, stinky balls from the back seat of your car. (A smell that somehow remains in the car long after the balls have been lost and replaced.)

You get to place responsibility for the most important piece of equipment on your players.

What I would suggest, if you decide to take my very sensible advice, is to have a hand pump. I hate flat or semi-deflated balls, and you can guarantee that a few of your players will show up with balls that feel like a wet sponge when you kick them. A properly inflated ball is vital to learning the correct art of passing, shooting, and heading. A deflated ball can result in improper technique. Bring a pump, and at $10 it's a heck of a lot cheaper option than a bulging back of wet, smelly balls.

Okay, so those are the basics of equipment needs. Now, of course, we can go deeper with agility, balance, and co-ordination equipment, such as ladders and hurdles, which I believe are very important in the development of players young and old.

A bag of free standing free-kick Dummies is another great investment if you can afford them. Although, they run into many hundreds of dollars, when one in three goals come from set pieces, they will pay for themselves many times over.

The Cheat List

When you prepare your training sessions always make sure you have a cheat list for what you want to work on. It's okay if you don't follow that list, as training sessions should be flexible, however, if you have a foundation, you'll have something to guide you if you get stuck along the way.

You don't need the printouts with diagrams that look like a design for NASA, however, they are readily available online through many different resources.

On your list, write down the important points of the session in terms of what you're looking to get across. Maybe it's controlling the ball with the instep or striking the ball with your laces, playing with numbers down, or possession in the final third – just make sure you have a few technical or tactical notes that will help you remember what you're trying to teach. Setting times for each exercise, drill or game will also keep you on task and focused.

It can be easy to get distracted in the flow of a session, whether it's moving along perfectly or you're having a rascal with players not listening and not focused. I hate the feeling when you're aware that maybe the session isn't working out quite the way it should.

After thousands of practice sessions, I've been in that situation on more occasions than I care to remember. You glance down at your watch hoping that you're 35 minutes in and 10 minutes have passed… yep, a long night!

A list can help you stay focused and organized.

Do One Thing at a Time

If you are doing a session on attacking using dribbling skills, don't coach how to defend against the dribble. I know it's very tempting to jump in and correct anything you perceive to be incorrect, but don't. Players have only a certain amount of bandwidth, and it's important that we get them to focus on the task at hand.

Don't go for overkill, though, and just teach attacking dribbling for 60 minutes. In my experience, 20-30 minutes is about the right amount of time to really push learning among your players and teach a topic. Any more than that and minds begin to wander, and the quality turns to mush.

Cutting a Child from a Team

In all my years of coaching, the one aspect of the job that I have never enjoyed is cutting players. Whether it is a professional whose livelihood depends on making a weekly wage or a young kid looking to get on his first team, cutting players is never nice unless you've been completely shorn of empathy.

Incredibly, this is something rarely addressed whenever I've taken a coaching course, and in my opinion, it should be one of the first topics addressed as it impacts kids, parents, and coaches for life as I'll explain right now!

When fellow coaches ask me how to deal with this aspect of the job, I usually tell them a story about the first coaching gig I had and a lad we'll call Victor.

To this day I still get a pit in my stomach about the way I handled cutting this young man, and will on my deathbed probably yell out for forgiveness and hope he hears me!

I was 23-years old coaching high school soccer and clueless about who I was as a coach and really as a person. I think the fact that I was only 5 years older than the seniors on the team didn't help as I was focused on being their friend instead of their coach.

It was the second day of a two-day tryout, and I'd whittled 40 kids down to 21 for the varsity team. I was happy with this, but during the session, I noticed that some of the kids were really flying into Victor with some over the top challenges.

To be fair, Victor would get up, brush himself off, and get on with it, however, at some point, he must've got hurt and started limping. I asked the captain from the previous year what was going on and he said that nobody liked Teddy and that he was going to get hammered all year long if he stayed on varsity.

Without thinking, I called Victor over and told him that he'd be better off on the junior varsity team and that he should leave practice to join the JV team on the other field... I feel like puking telling this right now!

I will never, ever forget Victor walking off the pitch to the other field, his head bowed, while the remaining varsity players took the piss out of him. I will never, ever forget him looking back at me with this expression of bewilderment, disgust, and shock on his face, and in his eyes wondering how an adult could be so insensitive.

Rest assured, my first high school season as a coach was a disaster, and deservedly so. It's one thing knowing something about the sport of soccer; it's another knowing something about a fellow human, how to connect, communicate, and have empathy. Yes, we have to make tough decisions, but there is the wrong way and the right way to go about making tough decisions.

So let's talk about cutting and how to do this most unpleasant of tasks in a way that is empathetic and more importantly, in a way that will keep the player in love with the sport or at the very least, still somewhat interested.

Other than serious injury, nothing is as traumatic than getting cut from a team. Players can experience a profound loss. Strong friendships are severed, and self-esteem is crushed as the bonds and uniforms that have come to define parts of their youth are taken away. The message that many kids take away from this experience is "you're not good enough, but, someone else is!"

When we look at the reasons why players are cut/released, I think there are a number of reasons.

The player isn't good enough for their current or future level and should move down to a level where they can compete.

Stakeholders within the team (usually parents) want to replace weaker players with strong players as a strategy to compete at a higher level.

The player has been injured and has been unable to recapture the performances that made them originally part of the team.

The player has behaved in a manner that is not part of the club/team culture and/or has broken rules that are not part of the club/team culture.

Not many will disagree with the removal of a player due to poor behavior, other than perhaps the player's parents, but it is far more difficult to handle the scenario where a player is not able to perform at the required level.

The following suggestions are intended to address these types of situations, so you never end up with a Teddy on your hands.

When you present your concerns to the player and their parents, always have a plan B that outlines what that player needs to do to improve their performances.

Listen, you're the expert, and it's your job to recognize what the player needs to do in order to improve. That may include clinics, camps, working on conditioning, kicking a ball against a wall, or working out with another team, just make sure you know what it is or at the very least get a second opinion on what path the player should follow next.

Please make sure, that when you present these ideas, you don't give the impression that if the player completes the following that they get to remain with the team. Players can easily put expectations into their own heads, and I can guarantee you that "expectations are resentments just waiting to happen" – with you on the receiving end.

Players need to understand that it is only by improvement and not, I repeat NOT, execution of the plan that will allow them to stay on the team. If you have chosen the right plan for your player, improvement must be the outcome unless the player has not worked hard or had zero soccer ability to begin with.

Players – and more importantly, parents – need to be kept informed of progress throughout the year.

Is the player getting better? What is the player getting better at? Are they not improving? Are they getting worse or have new problems come to the surface?

And I know this is a pain, especially for someone you're thinking about cutting, but do yourself a favor and meet with the parents and the player before deciding that the snip is necessary.

Next – and I've been guilty of this – don't drag the process out. The sooner you know in your heart of hearts that you've got to let a player go ... do it!

Let the player and the families know as quickly as possible. Whatever you do, don't hang out an olive branch of false hope. As long as you're honest you'll be the one who is controlling the narrative.

Sometimes it is hard to show empathy, especially to a child whose parents have been driving you crazy, but remember you can never take it out on the kid ... even though the parent may have given you multiple sleepless nights.

You should also attempt to never show emotion at this point unless it's genuine empathy, so having a poker face will serve you well. Eric Wynalda was great at this, especially on TV. He would wait until the camera was off him before quietly shaking his head when I wanted bailing out of a terrible interview ... thanks Eric.)

And I may have mentioned this before, but it's worth stating again ... formal evaluations at the beginning and especially the end of the season are your best friend. Using a company such as zoom reports make this process much easier.

You have this document in hand, and it is often the best time to cut players as it gives them a chance to work and practice during the offseason in preparation for finding a new team.

Advise a player/parent that the try-out process is going to be tough this time around and that they're not going to make it... once again, being honest is going to save you in the long run. You certainly don't want a situation where they show up to try-outs, and they're the worst player there. Kids know these things!

Never compare players against each other with parents either. This is a huge no-no and will create a monster right before your eyes. Players are always comparing themselves against each other as it is, which can develop into needless conflict if you're not careful.

It goes without saying that you should tell parents the bad news before informing the player if they are U15 and below. I firmly believe that once a player reaches 16 years of age, it's part and parcel of growing up and becoming an adult. Bad news is part of life and accepting things like this helps in the maturity process.

And to be fair, sometimes kids are smart enough to see the writing on the wall. I'm always impressed when a player comes up to me and says, "I'm not returning next season, but I wanted to tell you personally." That's class!

Admittedly that doesn't happen often, and usually, you get an angry voicemail or email, however, make an effort to reply and thank them for their efforts. You never know, the player could be a late, late bloomer and the soccer community is a lot smaller than you think.

As I've said throughout, if you're honest, it's going to go a long way. Now, I know we're all a little different and every player grows up at different speeds, but don't say "it was really close between you and X" or "just keep working over the summer and things will change" – own your decision because your message and how you present it will follow you.

If you're lucky, you might work at a club that has multiple teams in the same age group or teams in an upper age group that are at a lower level. If you think ahead, the smart move is to develop relationships with those coaches so you can trade players with each other.

Technical Directors love this as it keeps players and families in the club.

Have the coach come to your practice and introduce the parents and player. It shows that you're caring and thoughtful and keeps the player within the club. Nothing beats "we think you will enjoy this other team more, and you will probably get more playing time. You will feel better about contributing more. I was proud to recommend you to their coach, and he wants to see you at their tryouts."

On the other side of that coin I've worked at many clubs where coaches hold onto players they should move to a higher level team just because they can help their current team win, neglecting the player's actual development. Please don't be that coach. As soon as you see that a player has outgrown your team or age level, do everything in your power to move them on as quickly as possible.

At the end of the day, there is no easy way to cut a player, regardless of the relationship you've developed. I look at the professional game and top clubs release crowd favorite players all the time. It's just part and parcel of the sport. Sooner rather than later you're going to have to break some hearts.

Now thirty years later, if Victor showed up and the same scenario presented itself to me in the try-out process I would do things very differently.

I would communicate more thoughtfully and ask questions of all the stakeholders. I certainly can't change time but time has changed me.

Hopefully, these tips and tricks will lessen the pain for you, your players, and the people that write the checks, the parents.

Here is a letter I've used in the past that you may find helpful:

Dear David Beckham,

Thank you for participating in the 2016 – 2017 (team name) soccer tryouts. As you know, only 15-18 players were selected out of those who tried out. Unfortunately, you have not been selected as a member of this year's team.

I appreciate your hard work and dedication during tryouts. I encourage you to keep working and to try out again next year at (team name). It is not uncommon for players who did not make the team one year to keep working on their skills and make the team the following year. There are many ways to improve your skills, such as playing in the other organized leagues or by attending one of the many soccer camps that are offered in our area.

One of my most difficult responsibilities of being a coach is making decisions about who will make the team. We take this responsibility very seriously. As a person who has been cut from a team before, I know how you are feeling at this moment.

Please talk to your parents about times in their lives when they have worked hard for something that did not end up going the way they hoped. Sooner or later this happens to everyone. I want to remind you that there will be girls/boys playing high school soccer this year that received the same letter that you received today. Keep working on your game and good luck next year.

Sincerely,

Coach Webster

PLAYER DEVELOPMENT

Player development is one of the buzzwords most frequently heard in youth soccer today, but what exactly does it mean and as coaches are we responsible for it?

In my view, player development from U8 – U16 is made up of a number of things, and it involves teaching and facilitating the following...

- A love of the game
- Good technique
- Tactical awareness
- A desire to succeed

Love of the Game

Obviously, the coach cannot teach a love of the game, but it can be developed and enhanced over time. When I began coaching back in 1988, the first team I had was a boys' U17 team. They knew nothing about the history of the game, the star players, or even the major world clubs – except for one young lad, whose father was a legendary player for Manchester United. I won't mention names, but let's just say he thought he was the "best."

The boys didn't play the game because they wanted to emulate somebody – they played because they loved the competition and they loved to play soccer.

Nowadays every kid I know who plays soccer has heard of Lionel Messi, can do a trick by Neymar, wants to nibble you like Luis Suarez, and in the case of my son, watch Ronaldinho YouTube videos until his eyes bleed, but it doesn't mean they'll fall in love with the game. You have to facilitate that and create a platform without being overly pushy.

So how can you help kids who have a million other interests fall in love with something that their parents don't necessarily have on their TVs 24/7 except in the Webster household.

When I first started coaching at my current school the players would complain that the only soccer they could watch was on the Spanish-speaking channels, but then in 2000 that all changed when the Premier League came to Fox Sports World on a full-time basis.

Lucky for me, my players now had an excuse to watch the Premier League, as it was their coach introducing the games. I could immediately tell that there was more interest in the game, but more importantly, they started asking questions about why players did certain things...

"How come Beckham hits crosses first time?"

"Why are the Arsenal back four always in a perfect line with each other?"

"How does Gerrard run the entire length of the pitch, box-to-box, and still have the energy to play?"

With interest there was affection, and before I knew it these Southern California kids (who could name surfers at the drop of a hat) were wearing replica kits and talking about Thierry Henry and Roy Keane as often as they were mentioning Kelly Slater and his pals. This is where you now jump in!

You want to challenge your players to watch the best in the world on TV, regardless of whether its men's or women's soccer. With the amount of coverage available on-air and online ask your players questions about a game that you know is coming up. I wouldn't make it mandatory because that's going to guarantee that only half of them will watch, but I would frame it in as much excitement as possible.

The more our young people watch the game, the more they're going to fall in love with it. That's what happened with my high school players without me even realizing until a few years later when I instituted an alumni game.

I was blown away by…

How many former players showed up to play and they brought moms, dads, girlfriends, and in some cases their own children.

How many of them now watched soccer on TV as part of their viewing habits, including Fox Football Fone-In.

How engaged they were in who was playing where and doing what – particularly in the Premier League and La Liga.

How many of them said 'they loved' the sport and it was now on par with the National Football League in terms of entertainment and excitement.

Now, I'm certainly not going to take all the credit for why soccer's popularity had soared with my former players, but I do know that by talking about the professional game, having passion about the game, and relating that love to them through words and actions they had caught the bug. It's a bug they'll then pass on to their own kids, who will then do the same a generation later.

It is my belief that in the not to distant future, we will have an army of people who love the game, not just because they play but also because they idolize players and support teams from around the world. I also believe we're beginning to see this with the interest in the past couple of World Cups, although this is just the tip of the iceberg.

Good Technique

What is good technique? That is a phrase that I'm constantly asked about, and I believe it boils down to this statement:

"Good technique is the ability to perform a skill consistently under pressure."

So what are the skills needed to perform consistently under pressure?

- Ability to use both feet, to side-foot, and semi-side-foot the ball and kick it with the instep, both along the ground and through the air, over short distances
- Control the ball with body open
- Take and cushion the ball with all parts of the body (foot, thigh, chest, head)
- Juggle the ball with every part of the body (except the arms)
- Pass accurately from a standing position and while on the move
- Accurately shoot on goal
- Work on various crosses (whipped, floated, driven, bent)
- Learn the basic heading technique, without resistance
- Develop and stimulate body swerves and feints
- Learn techniques for taking a ball past an opponent
- Learn to shield the ball
- Learn to take a penalty

As you can see from this list, they all have one thing in common, **namely the ball**, so for those of you that believe in lots of running during your practices, let's change that scenario immediately. You can incorporate fitness in your warm-up and in game-like scenarios.

Of course, you can't develop these skills in your players overnight, as there needs to be a progression, however, by the time the players reach 14 years-of-age they should be adept and comfortable at executing all these skills.

Controlling the ball and first touch: Every player should be able to control the ball with the inside and outside of their dominant foot with one touch and also be constantly practicing with their weaker foot.

(Note: Yes, we love players with the ability to play with both feet, but let's be honest. If you have a child that is brilliant with one foot, think Lionel Messi, would you be harping on him in practice to keep plugging away with his right, or really refine that magical left wand? ... I think I know the answer.)

That means controlling the ball in a variety of ways, including on the move, flying through the air, on the turn, or any combination thereof. It also means that during the moment of control, the body is already moving into a balanced and controlled position for the second touch, which should be: 1) moving the ball away from pressure, or 2) creating a position to utilize a trick to deceive an opponent. The same is true for control using the thigh, chest, and head.

Unless you're a soccer genius like a Messi or Ronaldo, the only way you can master control is practice, and that is where you the coach/mentor/expert comes into play. Establishing a practice routine for your players outside of training is the quickest way for them to master a skill and generate a habit that if repeated correctly will serve them a lifetime.

Doing something daily can be perceived as a monster commitment, especially by the younger generation. That's why you minimize the task to just ten minutes a day.

I'm pretty sure that some of your players will do nothing, some will do the ten minutes, and for a few others, ten minutes may turn into thirty minutes. Whatever time your players do spend is progress. Slowly but surely they will improve until it becomes just the same as breathing, eating, and drinking.

Many times we dismiss, and here I'm talking about adults and kids, the pursuit of learning something new because the gap of where you are at now to the goal (which in soccer is something called perfection, which is reached by maybe 3 players ... ever!) seems like a million miles away. The key to progress is in small increments, and you have to be the catalyst for that.

The following is a list of tricks, turns, and dribbles that if learned and then mastered will help turn your players from good to special.

Turning with the ball: Every player who has made the leap to the next level – whatever that particular level is – has their "go to" turn whenever they are in trouble.

There are many turns out there, and I'll give you a list of my favorites and a brief description. To view the turn in action... visit our old friend YouTube, and remember – if you can't demonstrate the turn correctly then have someone who can, and if that person isn't available then have your mobile phone handy so you can show your players.

Cruyff Turn: Invented by one of my all-time heroes, the great Dutch, Ajax, and Barcelona forward Johan Cruyff, who dazzled the world in the 1970s. The Cruyff turn spins defenders right round and inside out. The change of direction and pace of such soccer moves can make even the best defenders look and feel like muppets.

The move is effectively executed when facing one way with the ball, taking it with the inside of your foot through your legs and back the other way.

When perfected, the Cruyff turn not only beats defenders but also helps you remain in a position to maintain possession by keeping your body between the ball and the defender.

Cruyff Turn Tips:
- Keep your body in a low athletic stance
- Make the turn quickly and sharply
- Big fake kick with the foot that will be performing the turn
- It's a one-touch turn… anything else, and it isn't a Cruyff Turn!

Roulette Turn: This turn was made famous by two of the greatest soccer players ever, Argentina's 1986 World Cup star Diego Maradona and French superstar, Zinedine Zidane.

The Roulette is essentially a spin move with the ball. It is a really cool way to change direction and create some space between you and the defender.

Teaching your players this move will take their game to a different level if they can successfully pull it off. One foot sits on top of the ball and rolls it to the other while spinning away and changing direction.

Roulette Turn Tips:
- Do it at speed, or it won't work
- The move is about body balance, timing, and footwork
- Keep your body low and use your arms to shield while turning

Inside Cut/Chop: The cut/chop may be the most basic move to beat a defender, however, it is incredibly effective, and every player should be able to replicate this move.

There are several variations of the cut, but the most basic is taking the ball with the inside of your foot across the defender, from one side to the other, cutting/chopping the ball quickly.

The move will work even better if you push it a little forward with the same foot you're cutting it with before executing the move.

Outside Cut/Chop: Use the outside of the foot to cut the ball back in the other direction. Plant the standing foot far enough away from the ball so you can pivot away, turn your hips and body, and cut the ball with the outside of the foot in one smooth motion.

Cut/Chop Tips:
- Setting up the cut is as important as anything. Open your hips one way and bring the ball across to the other side
- Execute the move quickly, or it will be ineffective
- One touch cut, don't over complicate a simple move

Rivelino Turn: Probably many of you who read this book are too young to remember one of my favorite players. Growing up in

Brazil in the early 70s, Roberto Rivelino was considered a god, especially in Sao Paulo, where he played for Corinthians, the main team in the city.

The Rivelino is a special move, however, it is also incredibly simple and very easy to learn. As you run naturally with the ball you fake running over it completely by stepping completely over it with the inside of the ball-carrying foot, then taking it with the outside of the same foot.

Rivelino Turn Tips:

- Set it up like it's a fake pass or shot, and the moment the defender flinches, you're off in the other direction

Drag/Pull Back: The drag-back (or pull-back as it's sometimes called) is the simplest turn in soccer and should be shown to players at a young age.

If you are dribbling at pace with the ball and you have a defender parallel with you who's about to get a challenge in to steal the ball, you can quickly stop the ball dead or roll it slightly behind you by placing one foot on top of it and dragging it back with your foot.

To break it down, place your standing foot next to the ball. Place your other foot on top of the ball (do not step over the ball and use the heel!). Drag the ball backward (maintaining control of the ball)

Drag/Pull Back Turn Tips:

- Make sure you turn your body the right way. E.g. if your standing foot is your left foot and your right foot is dragging the ball back, then you want to turn with the ball in a clockwise rotation until you are facing the opposite direction.

- Your second touch should be with the same foot and push the ball away, allowing yourself to accelerate.

Step-Over Hook: The step-over hook is another turn that can befuddle kids in the learning stage, but once they have it down it is highly effective in fooling opponents and creating space for yourself.

The idea of the turn (when done at pace) is to pretend you are going to pass the ball or dribble one way, but instead your foot passes over the ball and pushes the ball in the opposite direction.

To make the turn happen, you must ideally have your back to an opponent (or side-on in some cases). For a right-footed player, your standing foot (left foot) needs to be positioned next to the ball as if you are going to make a pass to your left. Your non-standing foot (right foot) will move over the ball (ideally at pace) and pretend that the pass or run is going to be made. Instead, using the outside of your right foot, hook the ball in the opposite direction to the fake pass. Follow your ball and the defender will be briefly following the fake pass, allowing you to get away. Just reverse the process for a left-footed step-over.

Step-Over Tips:
- In a game this turn must be completed at pace, otherwise, the defender will have too much time to see what you are going to do
- To make the fake pass realistic, place an arm out in the direction of the fake pass before pushing off in other direction

You MUST devote time to teaching your players how to turn with the ball, and if they show some talent with a particular move, encourage and nurture that until they can produce it flawlessly under pressure in a game or game-like situation.

Dribbling and running with the ball: I always tell anybody who will listen that running and dribbling with the ball is one of the most exciting moments in soccer. Think about this, do you go to the stadium to watch Messi or Cristiano Ronald pass the ball? No! You go to watch them frighten the life out of defenders with their ability to run and dribble at pace.

Much like turning with the ball, every player should have a move that they perfect, because it doesn't really matter if the defender knows you have it in your locker… if done at the right time, it's usually unstoppable.

There was a famous English player named Stanley Matthews who would terrorize defenders with the same move. Everyone knew it was coming, but in the old days of one on one defending without support, the poor full back would be toast.

I myself was never the greatest dribbler, but I did have a couple of moves that I would bust out should I ever find myself in the attacking third of the pitch, which wasn't often.

Scissors: Brazilian forward Neymar, who plays for FC Barcelona, is one of the best in the world at this move. It can be a deadly trick when trying to get a player off balance and you can almost cork screw them into the ground. The move is executed while running at speed, literally stepping over the ball in a clockwise motion with one foot or alternating both feet.

Scissor Move Tips:
- Execute the move at speed – NOT standing still
- Keep your knees bent, and body low to remain in sprinting position and easier circling of the ball
- Execute the step-overs over the ball at quick rhythm… slow step-overs fool nobody
- As soon as you have the defender off balance and at your mercy, push the ball by him

Heel Roll: This is a wonderful dribbling move that takes a lot of practice as well as the speed of foot and speed of thought. Zinedine Zidane was the best at this and turned it into an art form.

So here we go… take the ball with the inside of your foot (either one) across your body but not too far in front. Roll it about half way across your body then take it with the heel or back part of your other foot in the opposite direction.

Roll Heel Tips:
- Don't roll the ball too far out in front of you or you won't be able to get your other foot onto it.
- Soccer moves like this one need change of pace, so after you hit the ball in the opposite direction, sprint!
- Execute the move at pace while moving – not stationary if you want it to work.

Ronaldo Chop: As the name suggests, Portugal and Real Madrid superstar Cristiano Ronaldo has made this move his own. When completed successfully at high speed, it is a gorgeous sight. However, it is a tough move to master.

Jump with both feet and bring your non-dominant foot in front of the ball. Your dominant foot goes out to the side. Both feet come down at the same time. Your non-dominant foot acts as a shield between the defender and the ball. Your dominant foot will push the ball forward past the defender. Angle your dominant foot at a 45-degree angle so it pushes the ball going slightly forward, not sideways.

Use the Ronaldo Chop when you are running at speed, and a defender is coming at you from an angle or straight on. And most importantly, change pace!

Ronaldo Chop Tips:
- Change pace after you do the Ronaldo Chop
- Keep your eyes on the defender and not the ball

Important Note: We want to encourage players to do moves all the time, however, it's vital that the players know when and where it's most appropriate to produce the skill. Up until the age of U11, I would say anywhere on the pitch, but once they move to U12, attacking moves of this nature should be performed in the middle and attacking third of the pitch.

Passing and Crossing

The first three components of good technique (control, turning, and dribbling) have focused on what the individual can do. However, soccer is a fantastic team game, and very few players can win games on their own – despite what their parents might think – hence the need to be able to pass and cross the ball successfully.

There are many types of passes and crosses, but only those that reach their intended targets or are potentially good ideas are worthy of mention.

Passing: It is important as coaches that we teach the proper technique for passing with the instep, which is the most common type of pass. It would be taught like this ...

- Plant foot (standing foot) next to the ball first - this determines direction as well.
- The kicking foot's toe is pointed in an upward direction with the ankle in a locked position and heel down - using the inside of the foot (think like a putting stroke in golf).
- The player swings the kicking foot through the middle of the ball with the knees slightly bent.
- The key to keeping the ball going in the direction of the target is keeping the shoulders and head straight while leaning slightly forward.

Passing with the outside of the foot is a very tough skill and something I would only recommend for older players. I frequently see players attempting this skill with an unlocked ankle, which could lead to a nasty injury if an opponent mistimes their challenge.

Being able to pass the ball accurately with the right amount of weight and pace under pressure is the sign of good technique.

Crossing the ball: The ability to pick out your teammates in a crowded penalty area is one that develops with age. Young players don't have strength to fizz balls into the box like David Beckham, so you're looking for them to pass, however, older players should become familiar with this skill.

Pinging, curving, and fizzing balls is all about technique and timing. Only with repetition will a player be able to hit a cross exactly where they want, however with crosses it's just about finding a certain area.

Coaches love seeing balls flying across the top of the six-yard box, otherwise known as the corridor of uncertainty. It's the area where goalkeepers hate to go, and defenders usually are facing their own goal if they've been forced to turn. That being the case, you want your players to focus exclusively on the ball and the connection they make when striking the ball as opposed to picking players out unless they are completely unmarked.

Just like passing, you want to make sure you're hitting the ball below the midline with your non-kicking foot slightly behind the ball. By approaching the ball at a slight angle, you will be able to generate curve and whip. Your follow through should be fast and high, causing the ball to spin and hopefully dip.

As with all skill, practice, practice, practice.

Tactical Awareness

According to soccer journals, manuals, and the experts, tactics can be defined as the art of planned and rational play, adjusted to meet game situations in the best way possible.

In plain English, I think tactics means being in the right place at the right time from an attacking standpoint, and getting in the way and stopping your opponents from the defensive side of things.

By that reckoning, I believe that tactics can be taught because moving to the right areas of the field is something that can be practiced and replicated. Making the right decision once you're there is another thing entirely, and that is a talent which can't be taught… but it can be nurtured somewhat.

A player's tactical ability will improve with age as spatial awareness, practical application, and theoretical knowledge of match play develops through experience. Remember that tactical awareness is a result of the following: age, individual make-up, and the environment they play their soccer in.

The beauty of soccer is that there are so many tactical decisions to make and that the computer chip, the player's brain, must constantly be recognizing and using space on the field, whether attacking or defending.

The coach that can understand using space on the field and can teach that knowledge to his players is going to be the coach that change lives in terms of how players visualize the game. Once a player starts making intelligent use of space through movement and positioning, they become something special.

To back that point up, 98% of the time in a game of soccer lasting 80-90 minutes, a good player is only in possession of the ball for about 2 minutes, which means you're either watching the game evolve around you, or you're actually working hard off the ball to create situations that are beneficial to your team.

When to sprint, when to run, when to jog, and yes, even when to stand still, are tactical decisions that the brain must compute. And it doesn't end there because the running is not as simple as straight lines up and down the field. Runs need to be shaped and angled so as to open and close space, to lengthen and shorten, to widen and narrow the pitch, and to unbalance the opponent.

As a coach, you have to teach the quality and shape of runs that will keep the computer ticking over and not overload. You also have to let your players know when to start and stop running if they can't see it for themselves. I've watched countless players make 50, 60, and 70 yard runs that just weren't on in terms of the tactical design of the move and so a complete waste of time and energy.

On the attacking side of things, most players run far too early in their haste to get wherever they're going, while great players are the masters of the late run, ghosting in at the last possible second, making themselves almost impossible to mark. They'll begin their runs slowly before exploding in the last few strides. On the other hand, inexperienced players have already made their run and are standing still waiting for a pass or cross, making themselves easy targets to guard.

Meanwhile, as a defender, making tracking runs is much easier and could be described in seven very simple words... "STAY BALL SIDE NEXT TO YOUR MAN..." however there is a little more to it than that as I'll explain shortly, but first let's talk attacking runs.

The main factor with off the ball running is that players have to put their egos aside and realize that 98% of the time they are not going to receive the ball. Many times their hard work will not even be recognized, however, you can guarantee that if you don't make the required run, that's where the ball will surely end up.

So let's take a look at different types of attacking runs and see if we can recognize and then teach them, remembering that different ages see spatial relationships differently.

Penetrating runs from midfield and the back line are so hard to pick up, but they must be used through the lines of opposing teams. You can't make a penetrating run if a teammate is already in that space, and you certainly can't make that run unless you have the right balance in the team at that particular moment.

Third-man runs are all but unstoppable at every level. Defenders key on the ball and the supporting run, very rarely the third man run, which is usually done on the blind side. The best place to teach the concept of third man runs is in the early stages of development are at set pieces, where you as the coach has more control of the situation and pattern.

Checking runs are something that I think American soccer players will understand if you show them an example from the NFL. Tell them to watch how a wide receiving receiver makes a run down the line and then checks back to receive a shorter pass. Next, explain that they've killed two birds with one stone. Not only are they supporting the ball carrier, but, they've left space behind that a teammate could exploit.

Supporting runs to a teammate under pressure, recognizing that sometimes teammates can't see you, forcing you to find different space.

Overlapping runs are one of my favorite types of runs, as they require great timing and communication. I love watching a wide player drive inside, creating a beautiful channel for a teammate to run into out wide. This type of run is very difficult for defenses to deal with, creating unbalance and confusion.

I said that defending runs basically boils down to staying on the correct side of your opponent, but let's look at it a little more closely.

Recovery runs are no fun and occur on transitions. Your team is pushing forward, you're thinking of goals, glory, and then

BANG, your teammate gives the ball away, and now you've got to turn and start motoring to your own goal. Your first priority is to get goal side of any opponent and then think about where you need to be in relation to the man and the ball.

Closing runs should be described as closing sprints with exceptional speed, breaking at the last second as you never want to over commit and dive into a challenge. The quicker you can close down an opponent, the more pressure you're supplying, which invariably leads to your opponent panicking and coughing up the ball. The first defender, otherwise known as the player nearest the ball, performs this run.

Covering runs are performed by the second defender, who must provide support for the first defender, as we never want to see our back line in 1 v 1 situations.

Balancing runs are the job of the third defender in relation to the first and second defenders.

And finally, we have **stepping up and dropping off**. As my old coaching mentor used to say to me every day without fail: "we step up, so we can drop off" – what he means by this is the following...

Stepping up pushes our opponents back, which allows us to condense the field and support the attack, however by stepping up, we now create space behind us that we can drop into if we lose the ball and have to transition to defense. Stepping up and dropping off can be jogged, run, or sprinted for dear life.

With tactics, show your players through demonstration and video exactly what you want them to understand. If you explain it to them, they'll have a hard time conceptualizing space and remember, different ages will grasp ideas at a different rate of learning, so be prepared to be patient.

Desire to Succeed

What is desire? According to Webster's dictionary (no relation) desire is "to want or wish for (something): to feel desire for (something)."

So what should we understand when it comes to encouraging and igniting our own desires to succeed as well as our players?

Anticipate Reward

Be aware of the sacrifices and the hardships involved in becoming a winner (whatever that means to you), but focus on the rewards of success. Knowing what rewards you can earn stimulates your desire and makes you work harder for them.

Personal rewards could be as simple as helping your players in making a team to becoming the team of the year. Other rewards could be winning the league, state, regional, and national titles, and being recognized as a master coach in your area. As you can see, when you have success, your players will succeed as well. The two go hand in hand.

Learn Everything You Can About Your Goal

Read every book and talk to every expert, and more importantly, watch every video you can on the subject, whether it be defending or attacking.

Watch the teams, coaches, and players you want to emulate. Watch as many matches as you can live, in-person, and watch as many matches as you can on TV. Use my old friend YouTube, it is an amazing treasure trove of gold. You can find player highlights, full matches as well as coaching drills that often inspire me to develop and refine ideas, old and new. The more you understand your position on and off the pitch, the greater your interest will be. The more interest you have, the greater your desire to succeed.

Observe How Professionals Perform

Much like learning anything, really observe and take advantage of every chance you have to see and hear the outstanding individuals in your area of interest, in-person or on television. There are so many great books available that can provoke ideas and inspire you to experiment.

The more that you study successful players, teams, and coaches in action, the more familiar you will become with what it takes to succeed. Select a coach and study the progression and reasons for the success of that coach, you may start to recognize qualities that you both share.

I've stood close enough to Jose Mourinho to smell his minty breath as he conducted a Chelsea training session, and it was mind-boggling to me how much attention to detail he put into every aspect of the session. We're talking about the starting position of players, their body shape, and timing of runs... and these are international players who have won everything in the game.

Another coach I've studied is John Wooden. Yes, he was a basketball genius, however, his lessons on coaching apply to all of us at every level. In particular, I'm very fond of his coaching pyramid, and if you notice, the two bottom levels of the pyramid make no mention of the sport. Industriousness, friendship, loyalty, cooperation, enthusiasm, self-control, alertness, initiative, and intentness are all components for succeeding in life... and sport.

Constantly Remind Yourself of Your Dreams

Kindle the flames of desire and light the fires of enthusiasm by reminding yourself daily of your dreams. Envision the summits you can reach, the rewards you can reap, and the heights of happiness you can enjoy.

Strive continually to activate, nurture, and maintain the kind of desire that will make you a winner. For successful people intense, burning desire is a habit, a way of life, and a deliberate course of action. In any worthwhile endeavor, ultimate victory goes to the individual with the most desire!

That's how I felt at Fox Soccer and a major reason why I had the success I achieved.

Personality Formation

Along with the technical and tactical transformation of the player comes the development of their personalities. Many professionals I've interviewed were narcissistic and self-centered. I believe to become a well-rounded player and human being, such as David Beckham, for instance, you also need to teach the following while in a team environment.

- Teach players and your coaching staff a sporting attitude, in which respect for the opponent is central

- Teach players and your coaching staff to communicate with teammates and fellow coaches

- Teach players and your coaching staff to be open to the opinions of others

- Teach players and your coaching staff the finer points of leadership

- Teach players and your coaching staff to accept the referee's decisions… no matter how poor they think they may be

- Teach players and your coaching staff to be critical of their own achievements

- Teach players and your coaching staff to analyze their own game

- Teach players and your coaching staff to listen first, talk second

- Teach players and your coaching staff that football is a team sport

- Teach players and your coaching staff to concentrate on the surroundings

- Teach players and your coaching staff to be responsible for equipment

- Teach players and your coaching staff how to avoid injury

- Teach players to listen to their bodies

With all this in place, we can now charge forward to the next stage in our development, namely "growth" mindset.

GROWTH MINDSET

One of the biggest challenges and a question that I have asked myself frequently is this...

"Can I train my players to be mentally strong"

This is a question that many coaches, administrators, and parents are constantly dealing with. It doesn't matter how much talent an athlete has or how naturally gifted they are at a sport – unless that athlete is prepared to work hard and more importantly, fail, they will never have the resolve to maximize their talent and natural ability.

Recently I heard a story about Billy Beane, the General Manager of the Oakland A's baseball team and ironically a huge Liverpool fan. In fact, I had the opportunity to chat with Billy on the phone a couple of times when I was at Fox to talk about the book "Moneyball" written by Michael Lewis (read it if you can, it's brilliant) in which he was featured. He was a fascinating guy who basically redefined how baseball looks at talent.

Way before he became a genius General Manager, Beane was identified very early on as a baseball natural, and many baseball experts claimed that he was going to be the next Babe Ruth (no pressure, then!). These experts, didn't recognize the one quality Beane lacked... or more importantly, the quality he lacked didn't appear until the moment it really mattered. This quality was the mindset of a champion.

In "Moneyball," Lewis describes Beane in high school as an athletic Adonis. He was the top scorer on the basketball team, the quarterback of the football team, and had a batting average of .500 on the baseball team... however, there was a flaw!

He didn't know how to fail!

It was said that as he moved through the ranks as a baseball player, each at bat got a little more torturous because Billy never thought he should get out and that every visit to the plate should result in a hit.

Because Beane came from a place of natural talent and a "fixed" mindset, the idea that he could have deficiencies in his swing actually defeated him as a baseball player. His natural talent trapped him, however, he did manage to become a big time MLB executive. Certainly a case of swings and roundabouts if you can forgive the pun.

Now on the other side of this coin is someone who, like Beane, had outrageous natural talent and rose to the very pinnacle to become the best female soccer player of all-time, Mia Hamm.

When asked what's the most important trait for a soccer player, Hamm doesn't say dribbling skills, the ability to beat opponents, physicality, tactical or technical know-how, she says "mental toughness."

Can you imagine the kicking Hamm has suffered at the hands and feet of defenders whose sole job was to stop her by any means, fair or foul? It would be so easy to lose focus and start complaining to the referee, your teammates, and coach. Hamm acknowledged how hard it is to maintain that edge, saying "it is one of the most difficult aspects of soccer and the one I struggle with every game and every practice" but it is one she dominated because she has a "growth" mindset that was all about grit.

I'm no expert in this field, but Carol S. Dweck of Stanford University is. I've been reading and listening to anything I can get my hands, eyes, and ears on because I believe that this component – a "growth" mindset – if trained and taught properly, can set our players up for life in and beyond soccer.

Dweck has recognized the two mindsets ("growth" and "fixed") as the two hurdles that talented athletes must conquer in order for them to fulfill potential.

Think about this, coaches… how many times have you said to a player, "Wow, you have so much potential. If only you could do A, B, or C you could become X." Meanwhile, the player stands looking at you and nods their head agreeing, because they've heard that said to them many times over the years. In fact, I've lost count of the number of times I've seen unfulfilled potential in players. I've actually felt responsible for this on occasions, and I now realize I just wasn't speaking in a way that the athlete could understand.

Dweck says that those with a "fixed" mindset believe that their talents and abilities are "fixed" and what they have in the talent department is what they have. They are more concerned with looking talented and never actually fulfill their potential, whereas those with a "growth" mindset think of talent and ability as something that can be developed through "effort, practice and coaching."

Now, she's certainly not saying that we can all become Lionel Messi, Cristiano Ronaldo, or Mia Hamm, but what she does say is that those with a "growth" mindset understand that Messi wouldn't be Messi without those years of dedicated practice. According to Dweck, "in "growth" mindset, talent is something you build on and develop, not something you simply display to the world and try and coast on."

Great athletes never rest on their laurels, they are always trying to better themselves and take their ability to new heights. Dweck also says that a "growth" mindset creates a healthier attitude to practice, learning, feedback, and most importantly as far as I'm concerned, a far better ability to deal with setbacks.

How many times have you seen your most talented players lose their minds over the result of a game, their performance, and their teammates' performances? I don't think there is anything more cringe-worthy or embarrassing than seeing players bawling their eyes out, beating the turf, screaming at teammates, coaches, and parents, but it happens all the time because they haven't learned that to fail is to learn.

I know for sure that some of you reading this will be nodding your heads and saying that some, if not nearly all, of the best learning moments come in losses and in moments where you feel like you've truly failed. I know 100% that that is the case for me, and I also know that some of my proudest moments as a coach have come in those situations where the sting of defeat creates some of the best growing pains.

The next thing I'm going to say about "fixed" and "" mindsets is going to result in you going "thanks, Captain Obvious," however according to Dweck the one thing that separates the gods of sports, such as Tiger Woods, Michael Jordan, Serena Williams, and Mia Hamm from the merely talented and good is this mystical quality called... PRACTICE and another underrated quality, namely TRYING YOUR BEST!

Dweck says that the two mindsets work by creating "entire psychological worlds, and each world operates by different rules."

In the "fixed" world looking talented and cool at all costs is the goal, while in "growth" universe, it's all about learning and then learning some more.

Can you think of practices where you've set challenges that your talented players have gone through the motions performing because they believe that they already have it down cold? Meanwhile, your not-so-talented players are killing themselves to master this particular skill.

Perhaps you've set a challenge that gave your top players a choice of performing a skill that they've already mastered or a skill that they'll probably fail trying to complete... which one did they choose?

I think you know the answer! After all, who doesn't want to say "coach, look how great I am at doing a Cruyff turn" but this is fixed mindset. What we want is for our players to be striving for what they think is the impossible, "Coach, look how great I am at doing a Cruyff turn with my weaker foot"... now, we're in business!

In the "fixed" world, those with natural talent actually believe that they don't have to work that hard to attain mastery.

These are the players that have won or had success before with little effort while other players have to strain every fiber of their being to get the same results, however, these are often the players that never fulfill their potential. When they are asked to work at their maximum, they have no idea of what that is or what it entails. They simply cannot cope.

Those who have the "growth" mindset have already experienced hard work, they've pushed themselves to their maximum, and they've probably failed many times. They thrive on busting a gut, and they understand that effort is the key to exploring their ability and allowing it to grow and flourish.

This paragraph is taken directly from Dweck and should give us as soccer coaches pause.

> "Recently we conducted a small study of college soccer players. We found that the more a player believed athletic ability was a result of effort and practice rather than just natural ability the better that player performed over the next season. What they believed about their coaches' values was even more important. The athletes who believe that their coaches prized effort and practice over

natural ability were even more likely to have a superior season."

In the "fixed" world, setbacks can often lead our players to hide, and we've all seen players hide during a game. The field is massive, and there are 21 other bodies that can take attention away from someone who doesn't fancy putting him or herself in a situation where all eyes will be staring directly at the individual.

If a player is deficient at passing, then they won't look to receive a ball. Poor in the air and they won't go up and challenge for a header. Scared to shoot, which is the most common disease, and the player will look to pass instead. There are examples all over the pitch where setbacks occur and players will look to blame others for their failure.

In the "growth" world, your players keep asking for the ball, they keep challenging, they don't hide, they stand up and ask to be counted, regardless of how many times they fail.

You're probably thinking "Okay, Nick, we get it, but how do we communicate mindsets?"

Praise is the tool we use, however, it is very interesting to see how praise actually works in the different mindsets. Praising talent can make players feel defensive and vulnerable. I've seen it in my own child, who is just nine years old. Let me explain.

London (my son) has been watching World Cup and Champions League winner, the Brazilian great, Ronaldinho on YouTube since he was about six years old. Without any coaching from me, he has almost perfected the "snake" trick that the Brazilian uses to such devastating effect.

Now, of course, he can't do it at top speed or anything like that, but he's not afraid to try it out... unless dad tells him how great it is, and then he refuses to use it because he's scared to fail and mess it up in front of me. He doesn't want to risk losing the "Wow, London, you're awesome at the snake" label.

Bananas, right!? But a true story, so what I've learned – and it's been hammered home by Dweck – is that I shouldn't be praising the skill, but I should be praising the time and effort he has put into learning the skill. Bingo, light bulb goes off, music rolls... I mean c'mon, this makes perfect sense.

By praising the process of learning a skill, we encourage more learning, because that process really never ends, even if you're Ronaldinho. By praising the final product, we are shutting down the learning path, because what happens when you fail at the skill? You don't want to perform it anymore.

The "growth" mindset of effort actually encourages players to enjoy the challenge and remain motivated, even when there is a high degree of difficulty.

As coaches, we must put the focus on the process of learning and improving. This decreases emphasis from the finished product and the focus on natural ability. Setbacks then become a by-product of the learning environment and not what and who you are as a player.

Dweck also says, "Coaches can identify their "fixed" mindset athletes by asking them to agree or disagree with statements like this:

"You have a certain level of athletic ability, and you cannot really do much to change that;

"Your core athletic ability cannot really be changed;

"You can learn new things, but you can't really change your basic athletic ability."

Coaches can also ask their athletes to think about and complete this popular equation: What percent of athletic ability is natural talent and what percent is natural effort/practice. Coaches can then work on fostering a "growth" mindset in their players who place an undue emphasis on "fixed" ability.

Anytime you can ask players to complete surveys, honestly and from a place of love and care, you're going to get your players to buy into seeing themselves for who they are and not who they think they are.

And of course, while we're working on our player's mindset, let's not forget about ourselves!

I know in my younger days as a player and coach, I didn't want to hear what I thought was criticism, when in fact it was sound coaching however once I opened up my mind for "growth" receiving feedback became a welcomed component of being a great coach and better player.

I know that over the last few years my teams have, on the whole, had tremendous team work ethic and a real team spirit that we could call upon when the going got tough, as it always eventually does.

When your players know that you respect and value passion along with learning and development over talent, players will work together. One of the by-products of this may just be winning matches, or at the very least, competing at a level that you or your players didn't previously think was possible.

Ultimately, a "growth" mindset allows each individual to embrace learning, to welcome challenges, mistakes, and feedback, and to understand the role of effort in creating talent.

At the organizational level, a "growth" mindset is fostered when you and your coaches present soccer skills as acquirable through effort, improvement (and teamwork), and not just simply natural talent. We can then present ourselves as mentors and not just talent judges.

When coaching staffs have a "fixed" mindset, their job is to find the talent. When they have a "growth'" mindset, their job is to inspire and promote the development of talent.

I'd like to thank Carol S. Dweck for inspiring me on this topic, as I believe it holds the key for us in the United States to discover the next Lionel Messi or Mia Hamm. I believe that with 330 million people in this country, the next superstars of the game are not currently dribbling a ball on a pitch next to one of us right now!

Grit

Okay, so that's mindset out of the way, but what about this thing called grit?

Grit, according to Wikipedia, is defined as "perseverance and passion for long-term goals," while another definition I've heard is 'resilience under pressure.'

Our players and kids as a whole need grit, and I believe that right now as a society we are desperately short of this component in our lives. We all seem to want success immediately, or we'll move on to something else, but as a coach, we know this is not possible. As a coach, success usually only comes from "perseverance and passion for long-term goals" unless you are really lucky.

I would go even further and say that grit is a distinct combination of passion, resilience, determination, and focus. This cocktail of traits may just allow our players to maintain their discipline and optimism to persevere in their goals even in the face of discomfort, rejection, and a lack of visible progress for years, or even decades.

If our players have grit they'll work harder, endure struggles, fail/fall, get up, and try again.

So yes, grit matters, but how do we teach grit, if even possible, to our players when it's such an abstract idea? This is yet another question that coaches frequently ask me.

So let me give you an example of grit that I've used in pre-season training/team try-outs before. It's a pretty good indicator of who you want on your team when the going gets tough.

I call them "lung busters or gassers" because they remind me of the types of runs that full backs have to make if they want to attack and then defend.

I'll line the players up on the end line and tell them they have to do a certain number of full length runs in a set amount of time, which usually is about 10-minutes. If you don't finish the run, you're probably not fit enough for Varsity level soccer, however, the Junior Varsity team is an option.

The players begin running, and I'll call out the time elapsed as they pass by. As you can imagine, once you get close to the 10-minute mark, the physical nature of this running exercise is beginning to take its toll. However, the players think that it's almost over.

At that point, I'll tell them "another 2 minutes, and we'll be finished," which is where some of the players just collapse in a heap, while others continue on. I'll call the players who continued running back immediately and not say a word as no words need be spoken. We now know who will let us down when push comes to shove.

As coaches, we have to cultivate the desire and optimism that will allow our players to gut it out in those tough moments when it seems like you can't go on. We have to give them the confidence that they can do it and that we are supporting them every step of the way.

Grit experts say that there are a number of ways we can develop the right stuff, and it begins by finding your passion.

Hopefully, soccer is the passion of our players, but you might want to ask just in case, because I've met quite a few over the years who were playing to please a parent, and that's never a healthy situation.

If soccer is their passion, though, you must help them identify and understand that it is only through hard work, perseverance, and plenty of practice that they'll achieve their goals.

It has been said that one of the many characteristics of gritty people is that they are motivated to seek happiness through being focused on a task and developing a sense of meaning to that task. Like any task that requires attention, it really helps if you love and are passionate about that task, in this case, playing and practicing soccer.

At practice, you must require your players to work on something that is difficult. For some, that may be juggling, for others using their weaker foot. Try to set aside five minutes of every practice and then set homework that must be completed on practicing something that is difficult and doesn't come naturally. This is called "deliberate practice" and it's meant to be hard… and you're not allowed to quit.

This idea teaches our players to commit to the goal and to work hard at that goal. Learning isn't always fun and sometimes it may take weeks to see improvement, especially for young kids learning the sport. That said, if your players are motivated towards improving, then that struggle is as rewarding as the success will be. Practice, as we all know, begets skill.

As the coach it is your job to recognize when your players are getting frustrated at their inability to master a skill, however, this is where you earn your money preaching diligence and perseverance.

You need to be able to let your players know that the work they're doing now will beat out the naturally gifted players later on down the line, which is what I discussed earlier with the passages on mindset.

When we watch Lionel Messi slicing and dicing the best defenders in the world, it looks like the easiest thing in soccer, but we've never seen Messi beaten down, exhausted, frustrated or the years of practice and preparation that preceded the final product of him scoring goals, winning games, and earning accolades.

In describing grit, I have to mention the quote used in a marketing campaign by the clothing company Under Armour - "It's what you do in the dark that makes you shine in the light," because this is the effort behind the scenes that makes this kind of players shine on the biggest stage.

Last year, my son and I were outside the stadium at an LA Galaxy game at the StubHub Center in Carson, California, and this young guy, maybe 21 years old, was juggling a ball. His skill level, technique, control, and tricks were breathtaking, and London told me he wanted to juggle like that (his record then was 15 juggles).

London asked the guy how long he'd been juggling and he replied 16 years. He also said he'd been practicing at a high level for the last 9 years at least two hours per day. I told my son that was 6,570 hours worth of practice!

Grit also demands that our players take risks, and that means failure. Big time players take risks all the time and sometimes you have to taste failure before you can embrace success.

When I left Fox, the first thing I did was tell my son because I wanted him to see the fight in me as I moved onto another career. It wasn't easy for me to go from someone on TV every week to teaching in a classroom, but he could feel my excitement as I began a new stage of life. He saw my failures, wins, frustrations and happiness, commiserating and celebrate with me in a new and profound way.

The biggest thing I learned in that process is that failure was not the end of my life, and losing a job or losing a game didn't define me as a coach or as a person, and it certainly didn't define me as a loser.

If we have grit, we'll maintain our hope and our ultimate vision even when things look bleak. That is why we need to share stories with our players that don't always involve us walking off into the sunset with a trophy. Instead, talk about the times when we failed but showed up again the next day and more importantly, let them know that it's okay to fail.

I read a great New York Times piece called "The Secret to Success is Failure" by Paul Tough who says the following,

"It is a central paradox of contemporary parenting, in fact: we have an acute, almost biological impulse to provide for our children, to give them everything they want and need, to protect them from dangers and discomforts both large and small. And yet we all know — on some level, at least — that what kids need more than anything is a little hardship: some challenge, some deprivation that they can overcome, even if just to prove to themselves that they can." Just change parenting to coach and children to player and that's the environment we'd love to create within our teams.

Failure is painful and humbling, and as coaches, it is difficult to admit to our players that it happens to us too. Yet exposing them to failure may be the very thing to protect them against giving up when they come face-to-face with failure themselves. They need to know that frustrating and painful moments are not the end of something but a natural part of the journey toward achievement.

"Growth" mindset and grit are two amazing qualities that we need to have as coaches and two qualities that we must get across to our players, not just for soccer purposes, but also for the bigger picture of life. Yes, I know it is almost impossible to give a huge squad of 18+ demanding kids your time, but if you can change one life, then you have created something that could potentially change the world… and for this, I salute you.

Winning, Losing, & Everything in Between

Winning versus losing... ah, that old chestnut. This is a dilemma that at times is very hard to quantify and understand. At the end of the day a win is a win is a win and as the late, great Liverpool manager, Bill Shankly was fond of saying "If you're first, you're first. If you are second, you are nothing!"

The true beauty of this sport – and one of the reasons I love it so much – is because at times there are wins that feel like wins, wins that feel like ties, and wins that feel like losses. On the reverse side, there are of course losses that feel like a win, losses that feel like ties, and the worst kind, losses where you're lower than a snake's belly.

As a winner, you experience such a variety of emotions. To use a classic soccer cliché from the Premier League, you could be "over-the-moon," ecstatic, on "cloud nine," relaxed, buzzing, vindicated, humble, and even empathetic to the team you've just smashed 9-0.

As a loser, the emotions come even thicker. Gutted, shattered, depressed, angry, a failure, cheated, and "sick as a parrot"... I love that one!

At the final whistle when we cast our eyes around the playing field, we can find so many different emotional states. Both winners and losers unable to contain their delight/frustration and not afraid to share that feeling with anyone, regardless of whether they are a teammate, family, opponent, official, or anyone within hugging or raging distance.

So much of this emotion is dependent on ego, level of maturity, level of self-esteem, personality, and behavioral limits set by parents. Who hasn't seen players aged four to eighteen behave in a way that at best is embarrassing and at worst should get you locked up in some insane asylum with a straight jacket thrown in for good measure?

That's why as the coach and leader you're always a role model and should always try to set a great example.

Let's be honest here, if you've been coaching for any length of time, you know that this game will put you through an emotional ringer, because at its heart, soccer is a cruel, cruel game studded with the occasional ridiculous high and more often crushing lows. The emotional surge of a last minute winner in a tough game is matched on the other side by the devastation of conceding a last minute sucker punch in a game you've dominated.

These emotions are as powerful as I've ever experienced, and I've felt them rushing through my body at World Cup Finals and during my son's AYSO games down the park. Hopefully, I handled the emotional rollercoaster of AYSO games a little better than watching England lose on penalties in two consecutive tournaments to Portugal during Euro '04 and Germany '06!

These emotions – regardless of whether you're a player, coach, parent, or casual spectator – cannot and should not be underestimated or ignored.

Many participants know how to handle these epic rides, and their actions are usually classy and appropriate... however on the other side, oh boy, we're dealing with people who just can't handle these emotional waves.

They can become a tsunami of really poor behavior that is often inappropriate and infantile. Emotions control the way you act, and when we let emotions get the better of us, nine times out of ten the outcomes are sometimes not what we would be proud of in the cold light of day.

There is nothing quite like the guilt of realizing we've displayed really poor conduct when we've actually managed to calm down and finally regained our sanity.

So let's take a closer look at winning versus losing from different angles and perspectives, because it is important that we stand in others' shoes before we become the judge and executioner, starting with opposing coaches.

The Egomaniac

It's a little foggy after all these years, plus I've headed far too many heavy, water-soaked pre 1970 leather balls. However, I can't help but remember one of my first tournaments as a youth soccer coach.

It was one of those horror tournaments in San Bernardino, California, which if you live on the Westside of Los Angeles feels like you may as well be driving to the moon. At the height of summer, it's always hot out there, along with furnace-like wind gusts that would make a category 5 hurricane seem tame. Meanwhile, it's Arctic-like in winter.

I was with a brand new team of U12 boys, and we'd already played our first game at 8 am! Meaning I'd left my home at 5 am... poor me.

Game two was at noon, and I could sense trouble was brewing as soon as we returned to the field after a nourishing Grand Slam breakfast at Denny's. In front of us was FC Barcelona, well, an army impersonating FC Barcelona. All the kids were dressed head-to-toe in the latest Barca kit with matching Nike boots. The coach – who we'll call Coach X – thankfully wasn't dressed like Pep Guardiola (tight trousers, skinny tie), but he was barking out orders that would've put a marine drill sergeant to shame.

I looked at my players in their generic white shirts that were not nearly as cool as Barca, and gave them the thumbs up as they looked petrified staring at this mini Spanish army across the other side of the pitch.

As I always do, and I recommend you do the same as it humanizes you and your opponents, I walked over to shake hands with Coach X and establish some rapport. He looked at me as though I'd run off with his wife and ignored my outstretched hand while rebuffing my "hey coach, how are you doing, how was the early game, we're a new team just learning the ropes, etc."

Cue to the game, and within ten minutes it's already 3-0... to them. By half time it was 8-0, and my poor guys didn't know what hit them, especially from the frontline of Messi, Neymar, and Suarez, who looked suspiciously like they were eighteen.

Their bench, which was groaning under the weight of seven substitutes, several of who looked bored and frustrated, didn't move as Coach X began the second-half with the same starting line-up.

8-0 had become 13-0 before I'd had time to apply SPF 50, and he still hadn't made any changes, which by this point had begun to irritate me.

Meanwhile, my players' parents were all but ready to run across the pitch to start remonstrating with our opponents' parents, who were cheering each goal with a little extra gusto as they went past my beleaguered keeper.

Now truth be told, I had never been on the end of a waxing like this before as a player, let alone the leader of a team, so I was in completely uncharted territory. Up until this point, I'd fancied myself as a decent coach.

I had taken my USSF D license, I coached high school and had some success, but this was my first taste of complete and utter destruction... competitive travel soccer was something else.

I was wondering if Coach X was ever going to take off his MSN (Messi, Suarez, Neymar) forward line-up, which he finally did with ten minutes to go in the game of thirty-minute halves and the score 16-0. Eventually, the game that would never end was put to bed by the referee, and we did the customary high fives at the halfway line.

Now what I remember most from this embarrassing introduction to my competitive club coaching career was not the complete and utter hammering by an opponent. Instead, it was Coach X's attitude and demeanor that made this loss so "memorable."

As competitive as I was, I really didn't care that much that we had lost, because quite simply, they were better. I didn't care that we had barely crossed midfield throughout the match. The fact of the matter was that Barcelona was very good and we were very bad - plain and simple.

However, Coach X wasn't a very good winner. He wasn't a very good sport. He wasn't at all gracious. He didn't even try to hide the fact that my team being on the pitch with his team of superstars was an insult to his sensibilities and a big joke. He was a complete ass who openly poked fun at my team and me. And to add a little more insult to injury, as we shook hands for the first time after the match, he said with phony sincerity, "Gee, that was a great match your team played against me. You've got a good team." Note that he said "played against me" and not his team.

Coach X, in my opinion, was a loser with some serious self-esteem problems. At the very least he could've showed my team respect and kindness. He owed them some basic, common courtesy. He owed them a chance to lose with dignity. He didn't need his team to go easy on us, however, he did owe us good sportsmanship. Instead, what he gave my team was disrespect and embarrassment. His behavior was truly despicable and was not the behavior becoming of a champion. In my mind, it completely tarnished their victory.

We need to teach our players that you don't ever want to rub your competitor's face in his loss, regardless of how nasty this opponent may have been to you in the past or how desperately you wanted to beat them.

You never want to go outside of the sport to embarrass or humiliate your opponent in the process of your victory.

You never want to be disrespectful, regardless of your feelings about your competitor or the outcome. You want to keep your mouth shut and control yourself. This is even truer if what you have to say or do is ultimately demeaning or bad mannered.

Being a true champion means that you have to learn to conduct yourself with class, regardless of the level that you compete at.

Okay, I get that the world of soccer doesn't have the best role models at times. From Luis Suarez snacking on opponents' body parts to Mario Balotelli always making it about himself, professional sports stars can let their fame, money, and notoriety make them believe that they can behave in a way that is different to the rest of us.

To them trash-talking and ill-discipline are tools of the trade, or "part of the game," however I think deep down we know that they're acting like fools, and embarrassing themselves along with their clubs/countries and giving the sport, in general, a really bad name! This not what soccer – let alone any professional game – is about, regardless of the level. It is selfish and disrespectful to teammates and opponents.

If you want to be a class act, you must have respect and empathy for your opponent. Empathy is having the ability to step into another's shoes and feel exactly what they are feeling. When you can truly appreciate what your opponent is feeling, then you will be hard pressed to treat them disrespectfully. This is that basic "do unto others as you would have them do unto you" rule of living.

Simply put, you need to have a basic understanding and appreciation of what it feels like to be at the losing end. An opponent with empathy would never have done what Coach X did to my team because he would know that being treated that way by another coach feels absolutely terrible.

The Coach Xs of the world need to remember one thing about sports and life: What goes around will eventually come around.

Athletes and coaches who rub their opponent's face in a loss will soon find themselves at the other, much more unpleasant end of the game, just like Coach X.

So let's fast forward two years from this low point and back to good old San Bernardino, and who should my boys get in the knockout rounds of a tournament but Barcelona! Coach X was still there minus Neymar and Suarez, though he still had Messi, who now looked closer to twenty-four instead of fourteen-years-old.

Over the previous two years, I'd become close to my boys. We'd worked hard on learning the fundamentals of the game and played as a team. They weren't outstanding and didn't have the ability to take a game over individually, but everyone knew their roles and respected their teammates.

Coach X didn't remember my team or me, and he hadn't changed. By half time he was on the verge of a mental breakdown as his team was being outplayed, outfought, and outthought. To hear him screaming at young kids during that 10-minute break was to witness a very sad man, and you could tell from the body language of his players and parents that they'd rather have been anywhere else than here. They were broken.

At the end of the match and a comfortable 2-0 win for my boys, I was so tempted to say something during the handshakes, but, I had empathy. I didn't need to rub the result in his face as he was in a full on mission to do it himself.

Instead of handshakes, he was kicking balls, cones, chairs, and water bottles all over the place while using language that would've shamed a sailor!

Remember, coach's karma is always peeking around the corner in sports, and what goes around comes around.

Being a Good Teammate

A good teammate will be a friend for life but what are those qualities we look for when we are in those moments when being alone isn't an option. You as the coach need to introduce and develop the habits and mindset of being a good teammate because a good teammate is an incredibly valuable asset to any team.

A good teammate will always display the following...

Genuine commitment: Team players should always be committed during games and practices, however, great team players are always willing to give the extra 110%.

Adaptability: Instead of watching the team perform, an outstanding team player wants to make it happen through their efforts. They are flexible and can tackle new challenges without freaking out.

Communication: Great teammates embrace the idea of communication clearly and confidently. They don't stay in the shadows and hide from speaking their minds about issues that matter to the team.

Reliability: Who doesn't want to line up with someone who is reliable and responsible? There is nothing like looking around and knowing that your teammates will not let you down.

Listener: One of the greatest qualities anybody can have is to be a listener. This is a person who considers and respects ideas of others and is not wrapped up in themselves.

Helper: Don't you love it when your players help pick up equipment at the end of practice without being asked, or they jump in and help a teammate learn a new move or technique?

This is the person that involves all team members, not just the most popular.

Support and respect: Instead of shutting down ideas and making fun of teammates, great teammates know the meaning of respect because respect is only received when you give it to others. Great teammates know when to have fun but never at the expense of others.

Understanding the X Chromosome

Okay here's an interesting scenario for those of you with daughters who play this fascinating game. How many times have you heard the following statement uttered from your daughter's lips on the way home from a practice or game?

"Mom/Dad how come X hates me whenever we beat her/them?"

This is a problem that happens all over sports and in particular, female sports. As a coach, you better be aware of it, or you'll be blindsided by the ferocity that the problem can grow into.

There's no question that many soccer players – male and female – have trouble with losing. Losing is not nearly as fun as winning. Losing can be frustrating, disappointing, and downright discouraging.

If your ego or self-worth is tied up with the outcome of a result, then losing can be a big-time threat to your sense of self. In these situations, losing can trigger feelings of inadequacy followed by protective surges of anger and even rage.

Most serious soccer players hate losing with a passion. However, regardless of how unpleasant losing may be, all of us need to learn how to appropriately handle this sometimes unpleasant, albeit very valuable, common life experience.

As a coach of a competitive soccer player, it's partially your job to teach your players how to handle events that don't go the player's way. I say partially because some of the responsibility for imparting this lesson also lies with your players' parents.

On a girls U15 team I was coaching, we had a situation where we had a Blue and White team. For the sake of sanity we call them that, although everyone knows that's code for A & B.

On the two teams, we have girls who go to the same school and are really good friends... until they get to play in a match against each other. Let's call this young female player Jane and her friend April.

"Why does April hate me when I beat her?" Jane complained to me.

"We're supposed to be best friends, but after the match, she was really mean to me. She said I was a b***h and wouldn't talk to me all weekend. Then she posted horrible things on Facebook and Instagram about me. It makes me feel like crap and I feel like I'm doing something wrong. I mean, do I have to play badly, so she'll like me again? I just want my best friend back."

Have you had that situation before?

Girls competing hard against each other is what we're trying to instill, but it's one of the toughest things we as coaches have to try and at times, manufacture.

Society has asked our young women to prioritize socializing over being aggressive and competitive, as it violates the unspoken code of conduct, namely "acting like a girl."

In my situation, both Jane and April have entered this unspoken dynamic, with April slighted because she was outmuscled and outplayed, while Jane feels guilty for excelling and winning at a sport she clearly loves.

The truly annoying aspect of this confrontation was that the next time they played one another, Jane was so passive she hardly affected the game in any way for fear of upsetting her friend again. April knew what was up and you could tell was slightly annoyed at her friend for not trying while both sets of parents looked beyond bemused. Try sorting that one out!

In the interest of science and my own coaching sanity, I approached a colleague of mine who has two young women playing soccer and asked him about the unspoken double standard in sports: if being aggressive, competitive, and striving to be the best is considered such a good thing for males, why is it seen in such an ugly, negative light for young females?

Why can't girls and women feel great about getting stuck in, smashing someone in a tackle, and totally dominating a match-up physically and mentally? Abby Wambach certainly did this over the course of her amazing career.

If you work your socks off in practice and relish the physical side of the game, surely you get to enjoy and utilize the benefits during the game?

My colleague said that despite females being encouraged to be more aggressive and competitive, the bottom line is most aren't. It has not been fully ingrained in their DNA yet, Abby Wambach aside!

Winning still creates that internal conflict of being the best along with social acceptance, feeling good and of course feeling guilty. The by-product of this is that some feel wronged by the victor and act out in ways that with hindsight they regret.

As a coach of females, it's your job to normalize athletic contests. It's your job to create an environment where the girls can battle one another, push one another, really fight for the ball, and then at the end of practice be friends again.

You have to teach your players that it's their duty to play as hard as they can against each other as it's the only way they'll become better players. There should be zero guilt attached to beating your opponent if you worked hard and honestly to attain an aggressive attitude or exceptional skill level.

Now I'm not saying that you have to do this all by yourself, and you should definitely enlist the help of parents, however, you've got to recognize when it's getting a little nasty with petty jealousies rearing its ugly head.

All too often, girls end up acting out their feelings of jealousy. They get angry at their opponent/friends for winning. If a teammate or friend beats them, they may respond by ostracizing or socially punishing them.

I've seen terrible things done on Twitter, Facebook, and Instagram. This has been done whether the player exhibited this kind of behavior or not.

I've talked to many female soccer players over the years that were accused of obnoxious behaviors for one primary reason: They made the mistake of outperforming their friend or close teammate.

Working with parents, we need to teach these impressionable young ladies that losing is not a threat to self-esteem or worth, so as a coach you can't be upset when you lose a game. Practice what you preach and model the behavior that you want your players to demonstrate. If you see your players acting out in a way that you consider inappropriate to the culture you are creating, you must call them out on it, just not in public!

On the flip side, it's also your job to encourage your players to compete, play hard, and strive for excellence. It's our job to make sure our players never have to apologize for doing their best.

Soccer is the ultimate arena for young ladies to learn these lessons, own them, and grow with them.

Your Office

How many times have parents come up to you after a dazzling win and said "great game, coach?" I'm betting quite a few of you have heard this, however, how many of you have replied with "it has nothing to do with me, it was all the players' doing."

I've been saying this to parents for years in the hope that they'll understand when the shoe is on the other foot and we've just been hammered that they'll say "hard luck coach, your players were poor today!" Never going to happen, is it?

Now, how many coaches do you know who take credit for every little thing that their players do?

I'm guessing that every single one of you runs in the opposite direction when Billy Big Boots shows up. You know him because the first time things go wrong; he bashes his players and avoids taking any responsibility whatsoever when his team falls apart as they inevitably do.

It is always the fault of someone else. The referee had a shocker, the pitch was terrible, I was missing my best player, etc. The list of excuses is longer than Pinocchio's nose, and the attitude incredibly simplistic.

"Had you done exactly what I taught you, then you wouldn't have had any problems and would've performed the way that you were supposed to. The fact that you didn't is clear proof that you screwed up!"

...trust me, you never want to be this coach, and if you have a sneaking feeling you might be heading down this wrong path, it's time to change.

Think about what a nightmare it is to work with players who hold this kind of attitude. They've never made a mistake in their lives, and if someone should be held accountable, they are the first ones to point the finger of blame away from themselves and at everyone else including you, the coach. Whenever they do make a mistake they're ready with a litany of excuses, which they'll use with the skill of a trained lawyer, to take the heat off them and back onto their teammates and you again. They don't take constructive criticism easily, if at all, because they think that they are always right.

We've all had these types of players before, and they are a pain in the butt. Admittedly, some do change, but the majority remain un-coachable, and you're better off without them.

So now turn the table quickly and reflect that kind of attitude back to the players. Could you imagine playing for a coach like that? A coach who can't handle losses, a coach who can't communicate, a coach who looks at feedback as a full frontal attack on his character, a coach who above all is always right.

No one in their right mind is going to enjoy playing for that person, and if we're honest, that's the person that drives players away from the game, sucking out their love and passion.

One of the most powerful tools you have as a coach is empathy, otherwise known as the ability to understand and share the feelings of another.

The moment you take the time to understand what your players are going through and where they are coming from, you develop some serious allies. You will instantly become a more effective coach... I guarantee it.

When you are tuned into the emotional pulse of your players and team, you will help them feel understood, listened to, and, as a result, cared for.

Since the glue that holds your teaching together as a coach is the quality of the relationship that you build with your players, your concern for and sensitivity to where your players are emotionally coming from will help you build the highest quality coach-player relationship possible.

Stop and think about your experiences, your knowledge, and your skills. I'm sure they're incredible, but they'll only be effective and useful if you have developed real relationships with your players where they listen to you.

If you alienate and turn them off because of your impatience and disrespectful behavior, if you yell at them continually, deliberately play head games, or embarrass them in front of their peers whenever they make mistakes or lose, then they will not be able to use what you teach them. Ultimately they will lose respect for you and tune you out.

Losing a Team

Losing the locker room is a very painful and scaring experience.

I was coaching a very high-level girls U17 Premier team. 85% of them were college-bound, and we were flying near the top of the league, but then I let my ambition get in the way of my relationships with them. I allowed winning to become more important, and I can vividly remember the day I lost them as a team.

We were playing a team that we had comfortably beaten not more than six weeks previously, however, my attitude in practices and games had been worsening in the weeks leading up to this match. The pressure I had created around winning had started getting to me.

We had a free kick and my player miskicked the ball to our opponents, to which I cried out "we're the team in blue, they're the team in white, please for the love of God kick it to someone in blue!" – we never won another game, and I was sacked six weeks later… and deservedly so. What a clown, eh!?

What I had needed to do was look in the mirror and give myself a real good talking to. My ego, which was wrapped up in winning, needed to chill out. I needed to understand that regardless of level and ability, players will always make mistakes, just like coaches and just like real life.

Instead of using this opportunity to crush the poor young girl who had made a mistake, it was, in fact, the perfect moment to teach, have patience, and be a real coach instead of an emotionally out of control alien.

Having an awareness of how you internally respond to failure and then how you tend to overtly deal with it with your players will make you a better, more effective coach. Being unaware of your emotional responses will mean that the cycle will never be broken and you'll always be wondering why you've got canned from yet another coaching gig when you're actually a decent coach with the Xs and Os.

I get it that here in the United States the coach is God, especially in sports like football and basketball, however, let me take a quick timeout to borrow a phrase from those sports.

I was coaching the boys soccer team at a school where American football was THE sport, and as we're in different seasons, I thought I'd check on a couple of my players who were dual sports athletes.

The football team was having a debrief after a loss so I was waiting around to chat with my players about how they were enjoying the season and to ask what kind of work they were doing to keep themselves in shape for soccer when the coach went Mike Ditka on them (Ditka is a legendary Chicago Bears coach).

"You played like a bunch of girls out there," he barked. "It makes me sick to my stomach to even think that I have to call myself your coach. The bottom line is this, ladies: you totally stink, and you're not worthy of the uniform you're currently wearing! You proved that today over and over again. You're a total embarrassment to me, our coaching staff, and your school!"

Can you imagine being on the end of that? Yes, it was a big loss, but what can you take away from that emotional outburst? Would it motivate you, inspire you? Would you want to work hard for that coach? How's your self-esteem after that, your confidence?

Yes, it wasn't a great performance, and everyone knew it, but were there any lessons in that outburst that would help the players become better? Did they get information on how to fix their play for the future? Will they be inclined to listen to the coach moving forward or the tune-out process already be in effect?

I think we all know the answers to these very basic questions, but you only have to fly off the handle once to lose all the credit you've built up, and you just might find yourself dealing with players who fly off the handle at you because they've seen how their coach does it!

Now, of course, American football does have a macho culture surrounding the sport, but this is not how a youth sports coach should react.

Who wants to be known as the bully or the coach who exemplifies poor behavior. I get that sometimes we need a reaction from our players and I've even choreographed a meltdown or two however the ultimate goal is to be the role model you wanted your coaches to be.

So then why do some coaches insist on continuing to behave this way whenever their players fail? Perhaps some of this can be attributed to bad modeling. Maybe these coaches are just continuing to do to their players what was done to them when they were younger and played.

Too often this bad behavior comes directly from a coach's ego and self-worth being tied up in their athletes' performances. Simply put, when your ego is on the line every time your team plays, you won't handle losing very well.

Players need to know that losing is part of sports. Yes, we love to win, but we can't lose sight of "doing our best," because the beauty of soccer is that it doesn't always reward the best team.

A coach's influence on a young child is extremely important. The effect that a coach has could last for an extended period of time, far beyond the season. Therefore your personality, action, and words could have a dramatic positive – or negative – effect on each and every child. The value of understanding children, being fair and enthusiastic, as well as being a positive role model, cannot be underestimated.

"It is not up to me whether I win or lose. Ultimately, this might not be my day. And it is that philosophy towards sports, something that I really truly live by. I am emotional. I want to win. I am hungry. I am a competitor. I have that fire. But deep down, I truly enjoy the art of competing so much more than the result."

- Apolo Ohno (a pretty good skater, who won a few medals here and there)

WHAT IF THAT HAPPENS?

I love "what ifs" because we have a tendency to think they'll never happen, however, when they do, we better know the answers.

By the way, none of this is rocket science, but it is something called "common sense" and if we apply it we look like great coaches who are on top of their stuff.

Having worked in live TV, which I can assure you is stressful, I like to think I can "act on the fly" when something is coming down the pipes... however, it's even better to have the answer up your sleeve.

In the heat of coaching it's hard to think of every possibility, however, I'm going to present you with some "what if" scenarios. Hopefully, these scenarios will give you some answers that might help decrease the blood pressure in those moments when everyone is looking at you!

Meeting Parents and Knowing Your Coaching Philosophy

This is pretty much the first question I've heard at every initial meeting I've had as a head coach.

Do yourself a favor and have it printed out. It doesn't have to be War & Peace (a long novel), but it should hit some keynotes. It doesn't matter if it's generic, just make sure you believe what you're saying.

I remember the first time I was asked this question, and I was completely underprepared. Five minutes of pure BS later and I'd just about got away with it due to having an accent. The next time I had my philosophy ready and I felt like John Wooden

Do You Have the Practice Schedule?

This is always the second question because parents have schedules, and driving kids to and from practice can be quite challenging, especially if they have more than one child. Know it, and whatever you do, don't mess around with it once the season starts or you'll be enemy number one in quick fashion.

Do You Offer Financial Assistance?

This is more of a question asked in private, but the truth is that club soccer has become increasingly expensive. I've found that Financial Aid isn't such a problem on the girls' side of the sport, however on the boys' side, be prepared to get the checkbook out.

You need to know how much your club can offer because these are really tough conversations for some parents to have, as you can imagine. They want the best for their sons but may leave your club to find another if they can't get a number that works for them from you.

As we all know too well, it's the financial aid kids who are usually the most talented, which leads me to throw out this quote from a friend of mine ...

> *"No system of player development will ever match the desire to escape the barrio, favela, or the ghetto." Juan Arango*

What is the Registration Process?

Thankfully a lot of clubs have now have moved into the 21st century, and it's all taken care of online. Know the process, though, because sometimes it can funky, and parents will make you go crazy if they hit stumbling blocks.

Also, don't be shy in creating a Google document with phone numbers that are important in your organization. Chairman, Principal Technical Director, Athletic Director, Administrator, Accountant – these people should know the ins and out of the organization, leaving you time to coach.

Practices

Okay, you've met the parents... they love you and have entrusted their children to you for the season. Now the questions really start flying (just when you thought you were off the hook!).

If My Child Gets Injured at Practice What Do I Do?

Every coach's nightmare is to lose a player in practice, which is something that has happened to me with disastrous consequences.

I was coaching in the middle of nowhere and working with my goalkeeper on using her feet to combine with the back four when she stepped into a pothole and broke her ankle.

I had to get the remaining girls together while finding a pay phone (before cell phones) to call 911 while making sure that my goalkeeper didn't freak out too badly and go into shock. I was without an assistant, and no parents were anywhere to be seen. That's where you need a strong captain, and thankfully these girls were U17 and quite savvy.

As you can imagine, the second phone call to her parents was a brutal experience... and it wasn't fun when they showed up at the following practice to hammer me for allowing the practices to take place on a field that had potholes!

It was a huge lesson to me – I didn't have anyone to take over the practice, I didn't know where the pay phones were, and I didn't have a plan if someone got hurt.

When the next practice came around the following week, I'd already walked around the field and put cones down on any dodgy looking areas, had quarters in my sports bag, and knew exactly where all the pay phones were located. I also put in place something we called the parent tree, which entailed at least one parent hanging out in the parking lot in case I had to run off in an emergency.

The lesson was plan ahead and I learnt the hard way. If you're going to a location you've never been to before, get there early and get your bearings.

If I Get Hurt What Do I Do?

If you've been coaching as long as I have, then you're really old, and chances are you've twisted this and strained that. When I was in Florida coaching a decent U11 boys team one time, I had to take evasive action to avoid crushing a kid and rolled my ankle so badly I went into shock. I remember lying on the grass with a cold sweat dripping off me despite it being 85°+ and 100% humidity and then looking down at this grapefruit that had decided to attach itself to my ankle.

This time I was lucky in that there were a couple of other teams practicing and my colleagues absorbed my players into their practices. As for me, I was left to hobble to my car and drive home in complete agony.

What I didn't do, which annoys me to this day as I still have trouble with the ankle, is that I didn't report the incident to the club. I was a young coach and didn't want to cause trouble, but what I should've done is filled out an accident report and followed the proper channels, which in all fairness I didn't know that much about. If I'd been smarter and better informed, I could've got the proper treatment for those torn ligaments and I'd be a lot happier than I am now when it gets chilly and my ankle starts barking. Another lessoned learned!

Know what the procedures are if you get hurt.

Can You Adjust?

The players are at practice, they're fit, healthy, raring to go, and your session falls apart within five minutes because it's either too easy, too difficult, or they're bored. What do you do?

The first thing you must recognize is that it's falling flat. Nothing will sap the life out of you and your players than watching a disaster unfold and not doing anything about it. What I recommend is to get your players in a game ASAP, because after all, who doesn't love playing? This will give you time to figure out why you've laid an egg and adjust your session.

Most importantly, don't worry about the fact that you've had a rough one because players have such short memories. I've had some real rascals in the past, and they provide great stories later on in the season.

The Difficult One

The session is buzzing, all your players bar one are flying, but one is doing his utmost to **screw everything up** ... what do you do?

From my own experience, no matter what the sex or age, I have the player come and stand by my side and watch. You'll be amazed at what can happen when a disruptive player stands next to you.

They have to modify their behavior

They get to see the action from the coach's point of view

They get to watch their teammates having fun. It's a win/win, and within minutes they're usually desperate to get back in and knuckle down.

If that doesn't work, you may have to call parents and send them home!

Yes, not all children are the same, but it's important that you show consistency when dealing with disruption. If the poor behavior continues in other practices, you will have to remove the player from the team. It is so true that one rotten apple can spoil it for everyone, but be brave, strong, and committed. There truly is nothing worse than dealing with a nightmare child for a season.

Just recently I had a brand new U16 boys team, and there was this big, young lad. He was class. Strong, powerful, commanding, and someone you'd think you could build a team around. His problem... he couldn't keep his mouth shut.

Now, I'm not a big one for talking during practice except to set up the exercises. I do most of my talking one-on-one (and so should you), however, every time I addressed the group, the motor mouth would start with his act.

I asked him once in front of the group to stop. I asked him once privately to stop. I then told him in front of the group that the next time he interrupted would be the last time. A week later he was gone and guess what... everybody was much happier! I later learned that the previous coach had indulged this player because he was talented, but talent is never enough to conquer a motor mouth. Six months later, I heard he'd given up soccer to become a body builder!

Like I said, different players will respond to different methods and strategies. We as the master psychologists must figure out what buttons we can push and what buttons to leave alone. There is a certain amount of trial and error, but in all honesty, we can't afford to get it wrong often.

Game Day

Built-in excuses are a beauty for any coach to handle, and players of all ages love them as they are the perfect reason why a game has been lost The excuses usually start before kick-off, and I've heard them all:

Field size – too big, too small, too wide, too narrow

Field condition – turf, grass, rocks, dirt, weeds, potholes, etc.

Rain

Wind direction – Think Lancaster and San Bernardino in Southern California… it's always blowing a gale!

Sun – Think Lancaster and San Bernardino in Southern California… it's always hotter than the surface of the actual sun!

Referee, referee, refereee

Distance travelled

Games already played in a day

All of these require your attention, and whatever you do, do not buy into any of them, because you only have to let one thing slip and bang… you've given your players the excuse they were looking for.

Pre-Game

I love technology and having a team manager who does everything for me – including supplying me a nice hot cup of tea in the morning!

For those of you who don't have a team manager, I recommend an app for your phone, like teamsnap.com. It's super easy to use and pumps out maps, game times, who will be there, who's out, nearby restaurants, etc.

Always make sure you've got your forms (medical, waiver, rosters, player passes), because the one time you don't a "jobsworth" (a British colloquial word derived from the phrase "I can't do that, it's more than my job's worth," meaning taking the initiative and performing an action that is beyond what the person feels is in their job description) will be on hand to ruin your day and stress you out.

I know you packed the medical kit, but just to make sure, have a parent with a backup along with photocopies of the medical, waiver, rosters, and player passes. You'll be pleased you did.

Know the Rules

When at a tournament, **know the rules**. It's truly hilarious being on the sidelines when you know the rules and your opponent doesn't. Tournament rules change all the time. Goals are worth X, clean sheets are worth Y… you almost have to be Albert Einstein to figure some of it out.

I was at a tournament recently losing a game 2-1, and I knew that our one goal was worth an extra point, while our opponent had to beat us 3-1 for three extra points to knock us out. The opposing coach didn't know that, though, and thought a 2-1 win was enough. As they took the ball into the corner with 10 minutes to go, collapsed theatrically on every challenge and wasted time at every opportunity, I couldn't help but laugh.

Needless to say, when the opposing parents started screaming at the coach that they needed another goal to advance more comedy ensued as the opposing players tried to switch from being negative to positive. If only it was as easy as flicking a switch! Know the rules!

Uniforms

Here's another beauty I've seen many times in warm-ups: 17 players looking immaculate in their uniforms and one numpty who forgot his kit.

At the start of the season, I always request that we have one blank uniform. Your school or club administration might squeal about the cost, but it's going to save you a ton of headaches.

It's beyond annoying and highly irresponsible for a player to **not have their uniform**. In some cases, I'll not even mention that I have brought the spare along with me because players have to learn that their kit is their responsibility. There's nothing like driving two hours and not having your kit and then having to watch a game to make you more accountable.

And whatever you do in your entire coaching career, NEVER ask to borrow a kit from a kid and then give it to your best player who has of course forgotten his. I did this once almost by accident, and I'm still hearing about it to this day.

How many times have you heard the classic line… "I thought my mom" – oh boy, as soon as I hear that one my head explodes. All my players, regardless of age, know never to say that.

Blanks, though, are important as your players may get a bloodied shirt or it could be ripped during the course of a game, and we certainly shouldn't punish players for that.

I have the same kind of policy for players who forget their boots (sorry, I hate the word "cleats"). No boots, no play... simple as that, and players that borrow boots don't start, because I've never seen a kid play well in borrowed boots... ever!

I always have a spare pair with me as I'm a soccer nerd and will lend them out if a player's boots split, and the same goes for shin guards.

What you can guarantee about these pre-game "oops" is that only one in ten players will tell you beforehand, and in this case, I'm a little more forgiving for that one who has the guts to own up to their mistake. Most will wait until just before kick-off or when you spot the oops and then say, "I thought my mom!"

With every team nowadays having two uniforms, home and away, **color conflicts** are a thing of the past, however, they do crop up now and again. Hey, it's a good job you're a top coach and always have one/two sets of pennies in your car... right!

The Numbers Game

What happens if you or your opponents have an insufficient number of players as kick-off is approaching? In terms of nightmare scenarios, this one is right up there with the comedy own goal to lose a match with the last kick of the game.

When I've had the numbers and opponents, haven't, I'll make sure that firstly we've been awarded the win, and then offer to loan players so we can still have a game. I mean, why punish kids who have showed up?

On the other side of the coin, yes, I'm mortally embarrassed and hopeful that I've got a decent excuse, like traffic or illness. I'll suggest to our opponents to do the same thing I would do in that situation and lend me some players so we can still at least get a run in.

As soon as the game ended, I would be on the phone to organize a crisis meeting with the parents to find out what kind of team we want to be involved with because I have no interest in being left in that situation.

The Game

Blimey, by the time we get to the game we'll be exhausted dealing with all the nonsense I've just described. Hopefully, for you, those scenarios rarely play out, and you can enjoy the fruits of your labor in the stress-free environment of the game.

I may have mentioned earlier that it's classy and professional to seek out your opposing coach and shake hands before kick-off because it humanizes us. I know there are jerks out there that obviously have no manners because they're incapable of civilized behavior, but you just have to brush that off. They'll never change!

Marcus Buckingham, a self-help guru of sorts says the following...

> *People don't change that much. Don't waste time trying to put in what was left out. Try to draw out what was left in. That is hard enough.*"

I could say the same about my star striker, who refuses to pass the ball despite repeated pleas!

So we kick-off, and boom... big injury. It's just you coaching, no assistant, so what do you do?

Panic is the first thing that comes to mind because you've got to take care of your player while the game is going on. Or worst case, leave the game and head off to the hospital.

I've been in the above situation, however, I was lucky that one of the parents actually had his coaching card with him and the tournament organizers said he could run the team. If the parent didn't have his card, though, we would've forfeited the game.

Are you prepared for this? If not, find out how to prepare for something like this. What is your school or club's policy towards parents jumping in for you if you do not have a qualified assistant to take over? You have to know this, and I bet you don't!

What I would do just to cover yourself is have a parent (or parents) you can trust be ready to step in for you if a big time emergency happens.

Luckily for us, most injuries aren't of the broken bone variety, and with our First Aid certification and fully stocked medical kit in hand we're in control.

Game tactical decisions are all yours, and I would be a fool to coach you from this book, however, I will say always trust your first instinct and never second guess yourself. I've spent hours in the car driving back from matches and tournaments replaying decisions. What a waste of time that was.

During the game, though, the referee or officials might make your life interesting by tossing out one of your players and asking them to leave the field. If the player doesn't have a parent present, you can't really ask them to go and sit in the parking lot on their own.

Once again, do you have a plan for this unlikeliest of scenarios? When you do, you look like a genius… on the other hand, if you don't, well, the less said, the better.

The Fight

I've been coaching for four decades now. That's literally thousands of matches, and in that time I've probably seen less than ten full-scale fights. They're always a little scary because when emotions get that heated anything can happen, and we've seen from some horror stories in the news that the worst can happen.

Now in my book, to officially be a fight that gets out of hand there have to be more than two players involved because most two-person skirmishes are usually of the handbag variety.

Every now and then you will hear a play-by-player announcer (Martin Tyler is my particular favorite) say something like, "It's just a bit of handbags."

This is a situation where two, sometimes more, are pushing and shoving each other, usually after a bad tackle. "It's only handbags" means that the argument is not serious and should not become violent.

If you have a good, experienced referee on hand, he'll react calmly, probably dish out a yellow card or three, and tell the players to get on with it. On the other hand, if you have an official who wants to make the game about him or is a novice, and completely out of his league, I would expect to be finishing the game with fewer players than you started with.

Colorado Rapids v Atlanta Silverbacks

This is what happened when I was with Eric Wynalda on June 24th, 2014.

Eric, as is his way, called me the week before and asked if I'd like to go with him to Denver for the 5th round tie of the US Open Cup.

His Silverbacks were playing the Rapids at Dick's Sporting Goods Park. In typical fashion, he didn't bother following up until the morning of the 24th to tell me he was outside my front door and it was time to head to the airport. I threw some clothes in a bag and off we went.

Upon arrival at the team hotel, I bumped into some old Cal FC faces. Beto Navarro, Mike Randolph, Pablo Cruz, Jesus Gonzalez, and my old roommate Derby Carrillo as they had all followed Eric to Atlanta.

When we arrived at the stadium, Eric was filling out the team list and asked whether I wanted to sit in the stands and watch the match or hang out on the bench. I opted for the bench as I wanted to be close to the action, so he marked me down as an assistant coach.

The match began on a hot, humid evening with massive thunderclouds in the distance.

The Silverbacks were a decent NASL outfit, and with the Rapids going through a rough patch it wasn't a big surprise when Jamie Chavez, who I thought was a very good striker, opened up the scoring in the 21st minute.

The Rapids began to show their MLS class and were steadily coming back into the match when an incredible lightning show began exploding in the distance.

The referee made his only good decision of the night, and ordered everyone back to the locker room until it blew over. With just ten minutes left in the first half, the break came at a perfect time for the Silverbacks to regroup.

After a thirty-five minute break, we went out there to finish the first half, and it finished 1-0.

The second half began, and this is where the story really picks up. Twelve minutes in and Chavez made it 2-0 with a great header, however, five minutes later he got involved in a tussle with the Rapids' Marc Burch.

From my vantage point, it looked like Chavez stamped on Burch, which resulted in the said "handbags" as a number of players from both sides all jumped in.

Kwadwo Poku of the Silverbacks, who later played for NYFC, seemed to be in the middle of this pushing and shoving.

The fracas just kept growing until all twenty-two players were in a space the size of a phone box. It was at this point that our referee decided that the players should no longer be the center of attention and that he would like to take over as the star of the show.

Burch, Chavez, and Poku were all shown the red card. Wynalda exploded, walked onto the pitch pointing, shouting, and grabbing some players. Rapids Head Coach, Pablo Mastroeni, a one-time national teammate of Eric's, got involved and Guzman tossed both of them out followed by Eric's assistant coach, Ricardo Montoya.

The assistant referee then came up to me and asked whom I was. He looked at the team sheet and said: "you're now the coach, don't get tossed or you'll probably forfeit the game."

What! I'd only come to Colorado to give Eric some support, and now I was the coach in the 5th round of the US Open Cup with nine players. Only in America!

Nine players became eight players three minutes later as Borfor Carr got himself tossed out for calling Guzman a wanker for ruining the game.

This is comedy, right? So here I am, eight players versus ten, and there is twenty-five minutes left on the clock with a 2-0 lead. I shouted out to the remaining players that we'd play a 4 – 2 – 1 formation and just lump it long if we won the ball, and let the Rapids come again.

It was a classic offense versus defense drill, and as you may know, it isn't always easy to break down the defending team.

In the 75th minute, the Rapids won a penalty that Dillon Powers converted (no Cal FC luck this time), and it looked like it would only be a matter of time before the Rapids found an equalizer. Remember, we were playing at altitude, and the players were getting gassed.

I made a couple of substitutions with what was left on the bench and time slowly ticked away. As the scoreboard clock hit 90 minutes, the assistant referee held up the board for additional time. I was thinking it would be around six minutes because of the handbags... it was twelve!

Incredibly, though, we held on despite wave after wave of Colorado attacks, they just couldn't break us down... and to be fair, the players were heroic.

The final whistle blew, players collapsed to the floor, I unclenched my butt cheeks and ran to hug my old roommate, Derby Carrillo, who had done it again.

The Silverbacks had kept an MLS team at bay for thirty-seven minutes at altitude playing eight players versus ten... unbelievable.

Back in the locker room, there were great scenes. Eric (who had found a spot in the stadium to watch the match from) gave me a wink, and I called him a wanker for dropping me in it again. It was an experience I'll never forget.

Back at the hotel, I was too tired to even enjoy a beer. The mental and emotional work of cajoling and coaching the eight players had just shattered me.

A couple years later a US Open Cup historian put together a top 10 list of great Open Cup matches. Number 1 was Cal FC beating Portland, and number 2 was the eight man Atlanta Silverbacks holding out against the Colorado Rapids for thirty-seven minutes. Eric gets all the credit for both of them!

Anyway, back to handbags...

Handbags, in my book, is usually harmless, however, what do you do when it all kicks off, and you have a mass brawl on your hands?

Player Safety and Your Safety

Player safety always has to be your number one concern over and above everything else, and I think it's appropriate to physically drag and pull your players out of harm's way.

The problem occurs when you accidentally touch your opponents, and now we're moving into the land of assault. Whatever you do in your coaching career, please never grab an opposing player, because that will probably be the end of your coaching career.

At the first sign of a major dust up make sure your substitutes remain where they are and don't hesitate to say "if any of you step onto the pitch, you'll never play for me a." It has to be said.

Next, get in the middle of the skirmish, turn your back to the opponents, and start pushing your players back to the bench or your side of the field.

Unfortunately, you might get a few whacks on the back of your neck and head, but that's part of the job you didn't sign up for. The sooner you get players away from a striking distance with their opponents the better.

It's all about making a barrier and making yourself as big as possible.

Have your arms wide and make eye contact with as many players as possible. Do not focus on one individual, no matter how threatening they may look.

Now, it may be that your players started the incident, but your role is a pure peacemaker, and if you have the slightest concern that there is more violence coming then get on the cell phone or call for someone to dial 9-1-1 and get the police involved.

I'm sure some of you are asking where is the referee in this melee… well, it's been my experience that melees start due to weak refereeing in the first place. I sure hope that he's around to quell things, but don't be surprised if the officials are well out of harm's way on the other side of the field.

A few months ago I was at a tournament, and it was a very feisty match. One of my players was brutally hacked, much like Roy Keane did to Alfie Haaland (YouTube it). I ran onto the field to help my player when three of their players surrounded and starting pushing me. Holy crap! Now, I've seen everything – or at least I thought I had – until their coach started sprinting towards me looking like he was ready to rumble as well.

The official (who was barely older than the players he was refereeing) had lost complete control, but thankfully the linesman got himself in between, me, my player (who was laying prostrate on the pitch), their players, and the other coach.

I knew that if I lifted my hands there was going to be an issue, so I just turned my back on these lunatics, and that diffused the issue as they soon got bored swearing at someone who wasn't listening.

Still, it was a frightening couple of seconds and one that made me question why I was coaching. I mean who needs that? And to top it off they beat us 2-1 due to the fact that the referee added no time at the end of the game for all the nonsense, which eventually tabbed up to 15 minutes after the tournament organizers got involved and did precisely... nothing!

If a fight breaks out between crazy sets of parents, get your players away to the furthest point and **call the police immediately.** You do not want children getting involved in physical altercations with adults... period.

And lastly, document everything, and get your parents and players to write down exactly what they witnessed, warts and all. You'll be truly amazed at how people view things from different vantage points and biases. You'll be thinking were these people even at the same match as me, I can almost guarantee it.

The Man or Woman in Black

I've mentioned the referee in the last few paragraphs, and in these instances, he/she hasn't come off well, and for that, I apologize.

Refereeing is one of the hardest jobs to do in the world. I'm not saying it's brain surgery, but it comes a close second. I can say this because I've officiated matches and despite thinking I'm a great referee, I've still managed to piss off at least one team.

We all know that a referee will never change a call, and we also know that referees will make diabolical calls against your team for a whole host of reasons. So what can we do? Nothing... and that's why I love this game, because sometimes you have to beat your opponents and the officials, and nothing is sweeter.

Yes, you're going to feel sick as a parrot (to express disappointment at losing a football game) when you've been robbed, and that two-hour drive home is going to feel like six but trust me, it does all even out in the end.

If I there is one solid piece of advice I can give you and your team it's the following... remember the referee is human (meaning they're built to make mistakes), but find them before the game, ask their name, shake hands, exchange small talk, and tell them that your players will be respectful.

This is simple and effective, and it might buy you a call or two over your coaching career. Finally, no matter how crazed you may be, do your very best to find them after the game, look them in the eye, shake hands again and say, "thanks, ref."

Now if only our players had the same great attitude, but it doesn't always work like that. As the leader of young boys and girls it's your job to set the example, and if they can't follow your example then they shouldn't be part of your team.

My players get one warning when it comes to their behavior with officials, and if there is a second incident, unfortunately, they're done on my team.

At my high school that's a hard and fast rule written into the player contracts. My club teams don't have that rule in their by-laws and player contracts, but I enforce it anyway. You've got to have standards with officials because it is such a challenging position.

I'm not sure what I'll do should the next Luis Suarez show up to play for me, though!

Post Game

I just think that shaking hands or high-fiving with an opponent regardless of what happened, save for all-out war, is the classy thing to do. It sends a message that we can control our emotions and even grudgingly respect what our opponents have done to us.

Win with humility and lose with class.

Here are some favorite quotes that you can use that may help your players and parents take stock and realize that it is, after all, a game.

> *"The trick is to realize that after giving your best, there's nothing more to give… Win or lose the game is finished. It's over. It's time to forget and prepare for the next one."*
> *~ Sparky Anderson*

> *"Failure inspires winners. And failure defeats losers. It is the biggest secret of winners. It's the secret that losers do not know. The greatest secret of winners is that failure inspires winning; thus, they're not afraid of losing."*
> *~ Robert Kiyosaki, Rich Dad Poor Dad*

"Who apart from ourselves, can see any difference
between our victories and our defeats?"
~ Christopher Fry

Okay, time to pack up, go home, relax, maybe have a few beers…
not a chance, though, because on the ride home your phone starts
ringing immediately. Oh no, who did you piss off by not giving
them:

Any playing time

Enough playing time

Played them out of position

Shouted at them

Ignored them

I always respond with the 24 hour rule giving both myself and the
parents a chance to cool down however some are so insistent that
I'll answer questions 1 and 2 (regarding playing time) by asking
the following… "have you asked your child?" Invariably they
haven't asked, because if they had, they'd know the answer.

I'm very upfront with my players about playing time, and 99 times
out of 100 it always boils down to effort.

You can ask anyone I know this question… "what does Nick like
in a player?" and they'll reply "he loves a trier," so for me, effort is
the measurement stick by which playing time is earned.

Some parents hate hearing that because all they see is their skilled child who produces fancy moves, scores great goals, and provides assists... but never in their lives have they seen their child be lazy or not try their best.

As long as you're honest, your players should know where they stand with you. If they don't, I'm afraid you're not doing your job in the communication department, and you need to pull your finger out.

Playing them out of position can be a tricky conversation if you're not careful. After coaching for as many years as I have, I like to think that I can spot a position where I think a player will be successful. However, that didn't happen overnight.

I believe that up until fourteen-years-of-age players should be multifunctional and have the ability and the opportunity to play as many as three or four positions. Where that depends on the qualities they have. Once they hit the U15 mark, it's definitely time to begin specialization, and you as the coach better know where that is.

I've lost count of the number of players I've dealt with who claim to be strikers... except for the fact that they can't score goals! Don't tell me you've never met a defender who can't defend or a box-to-box midfielder who has an engine with a lifespan of about two minutes. These players are everywhere.

You must recognize qualities and put players in the right place to succeed. That may mean moving them around until you find the position that matches their tools, but as long as you let the player and parents know that this is how you work, you shouldn't get push back.

Being accused of shouting always makes me laugh and grimace – "Coach shouted at me!" Yes, coaches shout. Some shout absolute rubbish, some shout because that's all they know, and good coaches shout something called instruction.

Unless they've got bionic hearing, players on the other side of the pitch are not going to be able to hear their coach if he's talking in his normal voice. A coach has to shout… or as some of my players in the past have said, "scream," which strangely really gets under my skin as the thought of screaming at a child is something that I hope to never do.

I believe that if a coach is shouting instruction, coaching points, or encouragement, they're doing their job. On the other hand, if it is criticism and personal, that coach needs to have his head examined because nothing will put off a child from this sport more than a loud mouth obnoxious coach.

Ultimately you need to know your audience and how your players react to your voice. At the young age, if you start yelling, they'll actually stop playing to listen to you, which is a nightmare scenario. At the older level players may tune you out, which is an embarrassing scenario, so be smart and get to understand how your players tick and what they'll respond to.

The last number, number 5 (when a player feels you're ignoring them)! If you're ignoring a child, I'm not sure you're in the right profession. I've worked with teenage girls and boys and they can be really disagreeable aliens from a planet that you're not familiar with, but to ignore someone says more about you than it does about them.

Communication is the key component that you will live and die by as a coach. Knowledge, enthusiasm, and passion are fantastic, but if you can't communicate with your players then your time on a team will be brief.

Whatever happens in a game, look your players in the eye and acknowledge what they've done well, what they've done poorly, and what they need to do moving forward... but never, ever ignore them.

PROTECT YOURSELF

Dot the I's & cross the T's – otherwise known as the boring stuff that will sink you faster than the Titanic if you don't do it! Look after yourself and your players.

One of the most important components of being a soccer coach and one that was never imparted to me is PROTECT YOURSELF!

We live in a crazy, messed up world, and stuff goes down that you would never think possible.

And when I say protect yourself, you get to do this in a number of ways, so let's start with perhaps the most important way, namely insurance.

Get yourself some personal liability insurance. It's not that expensive, but it will save you a fortune when little Johnny was messing around, tripped on a sprinkler head, and busted his knee open. His dad – remember him, the dad that absolutely loves you, brags about you, tells anyone who will listen that you're the greatest coach since Sir Alex Ferguson – well, he's the one that's going to sue you and take whatever you have.

If you can't spring for personal liability insurance (about $350 per year), then join the National Soccer Coaches Association of America. These good guys provide one million dollars in general liability insurance plus a whole host of other goodies, including a soccer journal that comes seven times a year, an online resource library, coaching academies, plus so much more for the princely sum of $95... and yes, I am a member!

Find out what kind of insurance your school or club has and make sure that you know exactly what you're covered for. Knowing all this information will give you peace of mind because you never want to be in a situation when the phone rings and it's an attorney you've never heard of wanting to know what your liability is.

And don't let your insurance lapse. Tack a reminder up on the wall and pay those premiums or membership dues on time. You simply cannot afford to forget this because it has the potential to ruin your coaching career and your finances.

Now here comes the serious stuff... as a coach, I've always been the type that puts an arm around the shoulder of my players. I want them to feel connected to me, however not all kids like to be touched. In fact, many these days seem to recoil at that kind of physical contact... and that's just the males!

You need to let parents know from the very beginning that you may have to touch their kids during practice. I've been on my hands and knees before placing a child's foot alongside a ball to teach the correct technique. You may have to bang shoulders, lock arms, elbow ribs, or hold hands. Soccer is a close quarters physical game, and the last thing you want is for someone to say you touched them inappropriately.

I've been coaching girls aged U11 – U18 for years, and there is nothing more awkward than celebrating something with these ladies and the next thing you know they've got you in a bear hug. Try getting out of that!

You must learn to recognize when something like that is about to happen, use your best quick feet, get out of the way, and hang out a hand for a high five.

Trust me, people's imaginations can spiral out of control so quickly, it'll make your head spin. This is why you can never have one on ones with young players or girls. Always make sure that another adult can see any conversation so that there is no confusion and no grounds for anyone to accuse you of inappropriate behavior.

If you ever feel that any conversation is moving beyond your control, get out of it and make a note of who was there and what was said immediately using whatever tools you have on hand.

I know that some of you may be lucky enough to have assistants out on the practice pitch with you, and having that second pair of eyes and more importantly ears can be crucial, however, if you don't, make sure you're friendly with fellow coaches so you can look out for each other.

A tremendous resource I've recently been alerted to is safesport.org.

Safesport is an organization that seeks to create a healthy supportive environment for all participants through education, resources, and training.

They provide free toolkits in many cases that will give you guidelines to help you institute the right policies, and they best way to communicate them.

Everything is completed online and gives you an added layer of knowledge and protection. I would highly recommend every person who has contact with children to take these modules.

So now you've looked after yourself on the liability front, what about your own health?

One of the beauties of this job for me, especially living in Southern California, is the weather. Long gone are those freezing cold nights on Hackney Marshes with the rain coming in sideways and nowhere to change afterward. Instead, it's gorgeous 75% of the time, cold 5% of the time, and then seriously, blazing hot 20% of the time... however, the one constant is the sun.

Back in the early days when a bronzed tan was a sign of health, SPF-5 was the number one choice. However, by the time I'd hit 35-years-of-age, I was already going under the knife to remove crusty pieces of skin. Melanoma is no joke, and you can die from this disease. When you're out in the sun, slap on the highest SPF sun cream you can find, wear a hat, and wear sunglasses. You must protect yourself at all times. Just do yourself a favor and take the sunglasses off when you're talking to players and parents.

While we're on health, most coaches I know are in pretty good shape, however, it's something you want to keep working at. I'm no waif-like figure, but I'm happy to think I'm not the Michelin Man either. I know in the land of milk and honey it's easy to pack on the pounds, however, I always feel slightly uncomfortable when a clearly overweight coach is yelling at his players because they are not running.

Yes, we've got to look the part, which also includes wearing decent coaching attire. A stained t-shirt with last night's enchilada and flan still attached isn't going to win friends and influence people. A nice polo, sensible shorts, and team tracksuit top will give you the air of a pro.

And another thing, always make sure you have the emergency contact list on you. Sometimes when players get hurt, they get a little panicky and can't remember phone numbers. When players are in your possession, they're your responsibility and parents need to know that they can trust you with the most important persons in their lives.

On the subject of injuries, always notify the parents and your school or club officials. Follow up with written notification especially where head injuries and concussions are concerned.

This year for the first time US Soccer is banning heading from U11 and below with the following directive ...

In adherence to these new requirements, referees have been instructed by U.S. Soccer of the following rule addition: When a player deliberately heads the ball in a game, an indirect free kick (IFK) should be awarded to the opposing team from the spot of the offense. If the deliberate header occurs within the goal area, the indirect free kick should be taken on the goal area line parallel to the goal line at the point nearest to where the infringement occurred.

Now I'm not 100% sure I agree with this, especially as my own son loves to throw himself into diving headers, however, there can be no doubting the science. It appears that heading a ball before your brain has properly developed increases the chance of injury. So while I'm on the subject, let's take a quick look at concussions and give you some signs that you might want to look for if you've seen a clash of heads or a child has fallen heavily to the floor.

General Symptoms of a Concussion

- Headaches or neck pain that do not go away
- Difficulty in remembering, concentrating or making decisions
- Slowness in thinking, speaking, acting, or reading
- Getting lost or easily confused
- Feeling tired all of the time, having no energy or motivation
- Mood changes (feeling sad or angry for no reason)
- Changes in sleep patterns (sleeping a lot more or having a hard time sleeping)
- Light-headedness, dizziness, or loss of balance
- Urge to vomit (nausea)
- Increased sensitivity to lights, sounds, or distractions
- Blurred vision or eyes that tire easily
- Loss of sense of smell or taste
- Ringing in the ears

I know a lot of kids will say, "coach, I'm fine, put me back in" and I'll tell you now… DON'T … and yes, I am shouting.

If you have even 1% doubt, don't do it. No game is worth risking the health of a young man/woman or boy/girl, and I've been there with big matches on the line, and it's just not that important.

To be honest, I've been there as a player myself. There are matches I've played in that I've got no clue about because back in my day they'd drench you with the magic sponge and send you back out there.

I remember the beginning of one game I played as an eighteen-year-old. It was in the first couple of minutes when the opposition goalkeeper launched a towering punt. I went up to win the header and came back down wearing my top lip like a red moustache across my face.

Blood was pouring out of my face as the man with the magic sponge approached. He dunked the sponge in the ice bucket, rubbed it across my head and face, and as I recall said: "we've only got 11, so you'll have to stay on."

I have no recollection of the rest of the game, but I do remember going to the hospital later on that evening to have seven stitches inserted in my lip before returning to the clubhouse for a round of beers (or ten). We then drove home and off I went to bed. I love British medicine, but seriously…

My short-term memory is a little fried, and I put that down to the fact that we as players and coaches were not educated about concussions. It certainly wasn't deliberate, but we just didn't know… now we do, so no excuses.

Most players I know make good and speedy recoveries from a concussion as protocols are now in place… however, you need to take it seriously. You may think it's only a bump on the head, but that's all you can see, and you're not the neurological expert.

If you or your players start experiencing any of the symptoms I named above, get yourself off to the hospital, sharpish. I know it sounds a little over-reactionary, but if one of your players developed a brain bleed or other serious conditions, you'd want them to be in the right hands and not slumped on the bench in front of you.

Simply put, document anything that has the possibility of coming back and biting you in the arse.

The First Aid Kit

I can't tell you how many coaches go into battle without a first aid kit. I've been to so many tournaments, looked around, and unless they're hiding behind the boxes of donuts, first aid kits are AWOL along with the coaches' First Aid certification!

It is our job to make sure we have a well-maintained and well-stocked first aid kit. You can buy pre-made kits online or head down to the local pharmacy. If you don't want to splash the cash, then I can guarantee that your school or parents will chip in the money, because it's the smart thing to do!

What You Need in a Medical Kit

- Sports Safety Training Injury Prevention and Care Handbook
- Non-powdered Barrier Gloves
- Resuscitation Face Shield
- Cold Pack
- Bandage Strips
- Patch Bandage
- Elastic Fabric Flexible Bandage
- Kling Roller Gauze
- Eye Dressing Kit
- Eyewash
- Adhesive Tape
- Antibiotic Ointment
- Antiseptic Wipes
- Triangular Bandage for a Sling
- Insect Sting Ointment
- Hydrocortisone Cream
- "Save-a-Tooth" container
- Sun Block (SPF 30 and above)
- Foil blanket
- Insect Repellant
- Scissors
- Tweezers

And I would add to every game a bucket filled with ice, and of course, the "magic sponge." All these bits and bobs should store away in a plastic toolbox that is waterproof and latches securely.

Make sure you have enough supplies for more than one player, especially when you're at a tournament. Also, be sure to throw out anything that has an expiry date and has expired.

If you're smart and a coach that has a "growth" mindset, you will of course already have that First Aid certification along with your CPR certification. If not, please go and get it preferably after you've finished reading this book.

Hopefully, you'll never have to think of anything other than a few bruises and scrapes, but you never know… you might save a life!

Parents are also part of the first aid and emergency protocol, as they know what ailments their children may have in terms of allergies, asthma attacks, seizures, etc. It is their job to notify you in advance and not when everyone is freaking out on the field.

Make sure you know where those pesky medical release forms are. In the past mine have been located at the bottom of the ball bag, usually soaking wet and going through different stages of mold.

Get these puppies digitally recorded by a team administrator and on your phone. Now you have hard copies at the bottom of the ball bag and digital copies that will save your bacon just when you need them.

Here are a couple of sample player registration and medical waiver forms you can use. You can find them online – just remember to get them signed before you let the players do anything under your supervision.

Sample Waiver

Player Registration Form & Waiver

PLAYER NAME (PRINT)_____

BIRTH DATE_____

STREET
ADDRESS_____

CITY_____ZIP_____

EMAIL ADDRESS
(PRINT)_____

HOME PHONE_____CELL PHONE_____

PARENTS' NAMES_____

DOCTOR_____DOCTOR PHONE_____

INSURANCE CARRIER_____POLICY #_____

MEDICAL CONDITIONS/ALLERGIES_____

_____

In consideration of the benefits derived and in view of the fact that (your team/club name) is a non-profit organization, and that the participation with MVFC is voluntary, and recognizing that the sport of soccer carries certain risk and that every normal precaution will be taken to ensure the safety and being of my son/daughter, named above, in all activities of MVFC, I agree to his/her participation and waive all claims against MVFC, including claims against Coaches, Managers, Club Officials, Agents, Sponsors or other representatives of MVFC

SIGNATURE OF PARENT OR GUARDIAN_____

DATE OF SIGNATURE_____

Sample Medical Release Form

This form must be completed for each soccer player/participant under 18-years of age.

ORGANIZATION

MEDICAL RELEASE FORM

PLAYER'S NAME: _____

ADDRESS: _____

CITY: _____ STATE: _____

ZIP CODE: _____

BIRTHDATE: _____ GENDER: _____

DATE OF MOST RECENT TETANUS SHOT: _____

ANY KNOWN ALLERGIES (especially to medications):
_____
_____

MEDICAL CONDITIONS:
_____
_____

PRIMARY MEDICAL INSURANCE COMPANY: _____

POLICY NUMBER: _____
GROUP OR TYPE NUMBER: _____

PLAYER'S PRIMARY PHYSICIAN'S NAME: _____

PHYSICIAN'S PHONE NUMBER: _____

PARENT OR LEGAL GUARDIAN NAME: _____

HOME PHONE: _____

CELL PHONE: _____

WORK PHONE: _____

IN MY ABSENCE, ANY ONE OF THE FOLLOWING PEOPLE, IN THE ORDER IDENTIFIED BELOW, IS HEREBY DESIGNATED TO ACT ON MY BEHALF:

1. SECONDARY CONTACT NAME: _____

HOME PHONE: _____

CELL PHONE: _____

WORK PHONE: _____

2. COACH: _____

3. ASSISTANT COACH/TEAM MANAGER: _____

4. TEAM PARENT: _____

5. A REPRESENTATIVE OF THE ORGANIZATION WHERE MY CHILD IS PLAYING: _____

6. A REPRESENTATIVE OF THE TOURNAMENT WHERE MY CHILD IS PLAYING: _____

In my absence, I hereby give my consent and permission for medical transportation and to have a paramedic and/or duly licensed Doctor of Medicine and/or duly licensed Doctor of Dentistry provide my child or legal guardian, a minor identified as "Player's Name" above, with any and all medical assistance or treatment deemed necessary in the event of an accident, injury, or sudden illness. Further, I authorize admission to any hospital or medical facility for such treatment, including diagnostic procedures performed by licensed technicians or nurses. I authorize the hospital or medical facility to dispose of any specimens or tissue as appropriate. This release is effective until my arrival and its revoked by me. I agree to be responsible financially for the cost of each transportation, assistance or treatment.

SIGNATURE: _____

DATE: _____

Grub Up, Rest, & Drink

One of the most overlooked aspects of the game is nutrition. I've seriously lost count of the times I've asked my players whether they've had breakfast and lunch, and if they're hydrated properly and heard them reply, "no!"

It doesn't matter the age group or sex, for some reason, young kids forget that their body is a machine that needs fuel to run at its best.

It is not rocket science to say that soccer is a fast paced, intense, competitive sport, and the demands on a player's body can be incredible. During a game, a player is in constant motion for 30-45 minutes at one time, performing a variety of runs that range from jogging to all out sprints, followed by a 10-15 minute break and then another 30-45 minutes of constant activity.

The average soccer player can travel up to 8-12 miles per game depending on the levels they play at. This means that a great deal of energy and fuel is used and must be replaced, replenished, and topped up.

Nutrition needs to be the top priority of every athlete's training. What you eat daily, weekly, and monthly will affect your energy level, performance, and overall health.

Energy in means energy out! To perform at optimum levels a player must eat a well-balanced diet high in complex carbohydrates, and low in fats, which will help them to maximize their energy levels.

Proper nutrition not only benefits an athlete physically, but also mentally, and that's where many games are won on the field. If the brain is not firing, then the player will not play to the best of their ability.

Without the right food in the tank, a player can suffer from the inability to concentrate, lethargy, muscle cramps, dizziness, and in worst-case scenarios (which I've seen), passing out.

Playing soccer in Southern California, where temperatures regularly hit 100 degrees, we cannot forget about dehydration! A soccer player should start hydrating two to three days prior to games and tournaments. Good luck monitoring that, however, I try and get my players to send me texts and pictures of them drinking water during the week just so they start getting in the habit.

Players can lose as much as three quarts of fluid in a fast paced game and in hot climates. Fluid replacement is one of the most important nutritional concerns of a soccer player.

Young kids and parents are not aware that body fluids are not only lost through the skin as sweat but also through the lungs when breathing.

Fluids should be replaced during half time and if possible during the game, especially on hot days. Don't be afraid to ask referees if you can factor in a water break during a game, especially if the opposing coach agrees. This is for player safety and should be a no-brainer.

Liquids – and I prefer water to sports drinks – should be at or around normal body temperature, as cold liquids are absorbed slower. Water, along with sports drinks that may or may not be enhanced with electrolytes, is acceptable. Please do not let your players gulp these fluids down no matter how thirsty they are because the body will use and process smaller quantities more easily.

By following a good dietary plan, eating well-balanced meals, and staying hydrated, soccer players will learn how to discipline their bodies as well as their minds. If your players follow a plan, then their performance levels will increase, and overall health will improve.

I've included some information regarding the right kind of foods and drinks that athletes should or should not be eating or drinking prior to, during, and after games.

Please remember that this information is only a guide and there are no guarantees.

If you have any questions or health concerns, you must contact your physician or nutritionist as they are the experts and can offer alternative plans.

The most important thing to remember when developing a proper diet for any athlete is that it must be well balanced. Soccer players need energy for performance, therefore, the proportion of carbohydrates, fats, and proteins they eat is very important.

Having gone online and researched nutrition I'll break it down into the following categories for you:

- Carbohydrates
- Fats
- Proteins
- Vitamins
- Minerals
- Fluids
- Foods and drinks to avoid
- Pre-game, during the game, and post-game meals

Carbohydrates are fuel and come in two different types:

A. Complex = spaghetti, potatoes, lasagna, unsweetened cereal, rice, baked beans, peas, lentils, sweet corn, and other grain products.

B. Simple = fruits, milk, honey, and sugar. Complex "carbs" should be given priority because they provide 40-50% of our body's energy requirements.

During digestion, the body breaks down carbohydrates into glucose and stores it in our muscles as glycogen. When exercising, glycogen turns back into glucose and is used for energy. This is why you recommend your players to eat a high carbohydrate diet 2-3 days prior to a game or tournament so that the muscles and liver will store the amount of glycogen needed to sustain enough energy for 90+ minute games.

Fats also provide fuel for the body and may contribute to as much as 75% energy (why do you think I carry some extra around with me).

Trained athletes use fat for energy more quickly that untrained athletes and the amount of fat used as fuel will depend on the duration of the event and athlete's condition.

Stay away from fried foods. They will only slow you down and go straight to your hips and belly.

Everywhere you look these days, you see protein. There are bars, drinks, and supplements, you name it, protein is on it, however, athletes don't need to take huge amounts

Of course, exercise may increase the body's need for protein, but a varied diet with a protein intake of 10-12 % of total calories is sufficient because additional protein is stored as fat. Training builds muscle not protein. Some good sources of protein are fish, poultry, eggs, dairy, nuts, soy and peanut butter.

Vitamins & Minerals are also important, and if an athlete is following a proper diet and eating well-balanced meals, then these dietary needs will be met. Female players sometimes need additional iron and calcium. Iron can be found in certain foods such as lean red meats, grains that are fortified with iron, and green leafy vegetables. So eat your salads, broccoli, and veggies!

Calcium- Milk does a body good — the commercials didn't lie. The calcium, along with vitamin D, potassium and protein significantly increase participants' bone density — and a strong skeleton is key for any high-impact activity.

Get more from: Milk, yogurt, leafy greens, beans, fortified cereals

Fluids are just as important as nutrition and athletes need to start hydrating at least 2-3 days prior to competitions. Carbonated, high sugar, and caffeinated beverages should be avoided. So forget the colas, coffee, and crazy energy drinks!

Water is the drink of choice and the player should drink at least 3-4 (8 oz) glasses of water daily along with eating foods high in water content.

Drink Lots of Water. Remember that it's important to hydrate prior to, during and after games. Here's how you do it.

Pre-Workout Hydration

Before training, a match or a tournament, drink plenty of fluids. The day before a match, drink extra water, 100 % juice and/or other nutrient-rich fluids. Monitor the color of your pee, we want a pale yellow, not clear.

The morning of the match, drink 2 cups (8 oz.) of fluid two hours beforehand. This gives your kidneys enough time to process the liquids, giving you sufficient time to empty your bladder before the start of your match. What with nerves and everything else it's a nightmare if you've got to go and whiz just before kick-off.

Thirty minutes prior to the beginning of the match, drink another 5 to 10 oz. of water or sports drink. One oz. of fluid equals about a medium mouthful of water.

During the Match Hydration

Obviously half-time is when you take on water but if you can snatch a quick swig during the match, do so as you're losing fluids throughout the contest.

Post-Workout Hydration

After a practice or competition, drink to quench your thirst and then drink some more. Sports drinks are usually good as they contain sodium, which stimulates thirst making the player drink more. Just remember that the thirst mechanism is an inaccurate indicator of dehydration, you'll have to monitor the color of your pee to determine whether or not you've had enough.

Chocolate milk is another drink recommended by the USSF. Chocolate milk has double the carbohydrate and protein content of most drinks and is perfect for replenishing tired muscles. Its high water content replaces fluids lost through sweat, which prevents dehydration. Plus it provides calcium and sugar, additives that help athletes retain water and regain energy.

Match Day Feast

If you follow these guidelines, you'll be at the top of your game and then only have the referee to blame for a poor performance.

Eat a Late Breakfast

We all love to get some extra shut-eye, so if possible treat yourself to a couple of extra hours snuggling the pillow and getting tangled in the duvet. If you're playing in the afternoon, your first meal should be consumed around 4-5 hours before kick off. This timing gives off a slow release of carbs. Rye bread with eggs is always a winner in my books, protein pancakes or a bowl of tropical fruit. Try and avoid wheat and dairy as they may cause bloating and fatigue in susceptible individuals. If you can avoid dairy in the 24 hours before a game, all the better.

Go Lean at Lunch

What we want to do here is to top up our energy levels with a small, quality mix of carbs and protein. Small and quality because we want our body to digest this quickly, which thanks to the miracle of science, it does. Sweet potatoes or basmati rice with a small piece of salmon, chicken or turkey is hitting the sweet spot for athletes. But don't pile on the veg – anything high in fiber should be avoided unless we're heading off to the toilet Olympics. Keep fruit consumption to a maximum of one piece. You can gorge on oranges and fluids at halftime, but if you really want to be cutting edge Fig rolls are a much better choice as they are packed with both simple and complex carbohydrates, providing a footballer with a consistent amount of energy distribution in the second half.

Soothe Your Nerves with Yogurt

It's not unheard of to be so nervous before a match that you don't feel like eating. While understandable it puts you at a significant disadvantage as the energy tank will empty a lot faster than an opponent who has eaten correctly however if you can get a low-fat yogurt down your neck you'll give yourself half a chance. Yogurt provides a low fiber, slow release of carbs that your body craves.

Yogurt also contains a substance known as amino acid lysine, which has been shown to reduce anxiety and for those of us who are interested in losing that beer belly, burn fat more effectively than almost any other food. Yes, it's true! The International Journal of Obesity did a study and discovered that one or two servings of yogurt each day helped people lose 61% more fat than those who don't eat yogurt. Truly a miracle food, wouldn't you agree?

My final thought on nutrition is that we as coaches, players and parents do not take it seriously enough. If you can follow some of the guidelines I've presented, you will help your players and maybe even yourself in producing more energy, being more alert and hopefully having a healthier life.

The College Recruiting Process

THE COLLEGE APPLICATION PROCESS – SIMPLE TIMELINE

Before we really dive into the college process and the magical word of scholarships, let me just throw some realism at you. Yes, I know your child is the second coming of Cristiano Ronaldo mixed with a dash of Mia Hamm, and a full ride is a slam-dunk but for the rest of you, read on!

The chances of earning a NCAA sports scholarship are not good. In fact, only about 2 percent of high school athletes win sports scholarships every year at NCAA colleges and universities. Yes, you might as well head to Vegas and put it all on red. For those who do have the skill and luck to be in the right place at the right time, the average scholarship is less than $11,000.

Full-ride sports scholarships are like the 209 bus I rode to school every day... they don't come around that often. There are only six sports where all the scholarships are a full ride. Those six are the following: football, men and women's basketball, women's gymnastics, volleyball, and tennis. In these Division 1 sports, athletes receive a full-ride or no ride. Sorry, soccer players.

Scholarships can be tiny. All other sports are considered "equivalency" sports. NCAA rules dictate how much money a program, such as lacrosse or track, can spend on scholarships. Coaches can slice and dice these awards as they choose, which can lead to awfully small scholarships.

Take flattery with a grain of salt. Coaches may tell teenagers that they have lots of scholarship money to divvy out. What really matters is the scholarship amount contained in the school's official athletic grant-in-aid form. Until you get the grant-in-aid form, you better hope that the stories of your uncle's will and the colleges money are true.

A verbal commitment is meaningless. I've heard of coaches telling athletes as young as seventh-graders that they want them for their team. There is no guarantee that a child who verbally commits to a team will end up on it. A coach can change his mind about a prospect.

Playing high-level college sports will be a full-time job. Division 1 athletes may as well be called full-time employees of their schools because of the long hours they work. According to a recent NCAA survey, playing football required 43.3 hours per week; college baseball, 42.1 hours; men's basketball, 39.2 hours; and women's basketball, 37.6 hours. Because of the huge time commitment, as well as time away from campus, Division I athletes will often not be able to major in rigorous disciplines, such as the sciences and engineering.

Skip hiring an athletic recruiter. Coaches don't want recruiters to get in the middle; they prefer direct dealings with the student athletes.

Forget about slick videos. Coaches don't want athletes to send lengthy videos. Two or three minutes will usually suffice. And you absolutely don't need to hire a professional to do the filming. Post your action video on YouTube and send coaches the link. Better yet, use vLoop, it's free, easy, and can really highlight your particular skillset.

Okay, now I've shattered your dreams of saving $250K, here's how you can end up getting your superstar player into college and playing the sport that they love.

This chapter will give your kids a guideline as to what they should be looking for and preparing in order to make the right decisions as they look at colleges. In order to turn our dreams into reality, we have to look at this process as a military operation and be extremely organized.

Like all attempts to improve and better our lives, stress and pressure definitely enter the equation. Don't be surprised when your child snaps and tells you where to shove it, however if we follow these simple rules, ultimately whether we are successful or not, we'll know we've done our best. So put on your Sunday best and be personable, professional, and most importantly, persistent.

If you're a freshman, you should be watching and supporting your local colleges. Firstly, it's the right thing to do, and secondly, if you stay local, you'll save your parents a fortune. Watch all levels from Junior College to Division 1. Since most college facilities/stadiums are small, coaches and players will soon recognize you. Before you know it, you'll probably be the mascot, or at the very least a ball boy/girl, and this will give you a good feel for how competitive the game is and whether you'll be up for that in four years time.

If you've got brothers and sisters already in college, go and visit them if they're out of state, as this will give you a sense of what college life is all about. And then worst case scenario, have your parents take you on a college trip over the summer or Spring Break.

You definitely want to get a feel for the type of college that you want to attend. Big city, small campus, huge college, big campus, small town, etc.

Once you have an idea of what type and size of school you would like to attend, it's time to focus on the most important component... and that's grades, because unless you're Lionel Messi, your soccer ability carries no weight, but if you're the same ability as the next person and they have A's, you might get aced. The competition for college placement is fierce, so you constantly have to be working on both sides of your game: soccer and schoolwork!

It goes without saying that at this stage of a player's development that they're constantly working on the technical, tactical, physical, and psychological components.

Every game and practice you participate in becomes an opportunity to practice your game to the best of your abilities while acquiring the four qualities needed to succeed, namely ability, desire, luck, and nerve.

As a sophomore in high school, you should be doing all of the above plus compiling a dossier of the schools you like. There is no excuse for not going online and knowing everything there is to know about a particular program. This is what kids do if they truly want to be admitted to a particular institution... you can't leave it to chance.

You'll also have a good idea as to who you are as a player by this point. This will help you in narrowing down the level you can play at, so please be realistic. You can't shoot for Division 1 if you don't have the ability to compete at this level, and in all honesty, if you do have this ability, college coaches will already be sniffing around.

Most importantly, imagine yourself at this school as a student, not just a soccer player, because crazy stuff happens all the time. You might fall out with the coach, fall out of love with the game, realize that school life is more important to you, or the worst-case scenario, suffer a career ending injury. If you love the institution you're at, it'll soften the blow, and you'll probably have a great support system around you.

As that particular soccer season progresses at the program of your dreams, make a note of who is playing where and what kind of minutes they're getting, because you'll not want to be a freshman up against a four-year senior as your chances of playing time will be significantly impacted.

Okay, you've been diligent and attended games, you've compiled your dossier, you know who is in and who will be out. It's your junior year, and everything is on the line.

By this stage of your research, you should have a list of 15-25 colleges that you think could be a good fit for you. That list will be broken down into "must go there," "like it," and "if I had to, it wouldn't be the worst," along with their admission requirements and whether it's financially possible.

At this point you want your club coaches or College Liaison Specialist at high school to work with you on narrowing down your list based on your desires. If they feel a certain program would not be right for you, or too much of a high expectation, they should be honest in letting you know.

Prepare cover letter/email, profile, and schedule. Later in this packet, you will find a template letter. Start to use this template as your first point of communication with college coaches.

Remember, there will be hundreds of other players emailing the same exact college coaches, so you need to assume that your email/letter going into the "maybe" pile, so it'll take work and persistence to go from the "maybe" pile to the "accepted" pile.

Along with your cover letter, you should send the coach a one-page bio, including height, weight, grades, school, AP classes you may be taking, jersey number, and soccer achievements.

The final piece to the introduction email/letter should be your upcoming schedule. List upcoming tournaments you will attend and any league games you have coming up.

You may be sending out the same cover letter/email up to 30 times, so it is VERY IMPORTANT you read through before you send. Make sure you have changed the college name, coach's name, and the spelling is accurate. It is also a good idea to open the letter with acknowledgment of the soccer program, or any player highlights.

For example...

> Dear Coach Webster,
>
> My name is Lionel Messi, I am a center forward for the U17 Argentina National Team and have a strong interest in your program. Before I tell you more about myself I wanted to congratulate you on the win this past weekend, I noticed Amy Wambach scored again making her the highest scorer in the ACC. I am looking forward to seeing your team play on October 15th against UNC.

This shows the coach you have been following the program, players, and have a strong interest. College coaches receive a lot of bulk, general emails with no signs of real interest, and often still have a different coach or school name because the sender forgot to make the edits. Be VERY careful with this and make sure you know about their program. The persistence starts now!

Follow up with a phone call to the coach; make sure they have received your email, bio and schedule and spend some time talking about their program and how you feel you would be a good fit.

NOTE: It is VERY rare that you make one phone call and a coach picks up or returns your call straight away. College coaches are very busy, especially during the season, and this is where persistence pays off. If they do not answer or do not call you back immediately, do not panic... just keep being persistent. It is like a sales job, and you are the product being sold.

ADVICE: Rehearse phone calls, especially when leaving messages. Your message should be clear and confident. Leave your name, club, high school, and note that you are following up on the bio you emailed them on a specific date. Also, let them know when you will call back. College coaches are not allowed to contact you until September 1st of your junior year. Before that, you can contact them, however, they cannot contact you directly.

Here is an example message:

> Hello Coach Webster, this is Lionel Messi from the U17 national team calling on Monday, January 2nd. I was calling to confirm you received the email and bio I sent on Monday, December 25th.
>
> I am very interested in your program and would like to speak to you in person to discuss me as a player and how I believe I can be beneficial to your program. I will try calling back again today at 4 pm, if I don't get a hold of

you I will try again tomorrow at 11 am. I look forward to speaking with you soon.

DO NOT think one phone call will suffice, you may need to make 5-10 phone calls before you and the college coach connect. The more persistent you are with your calls, the more known your name will become to the coach. This is one way you can jump from the "maybe" pile to the "accepted" pile.

NOTE: your club coach or College Liaison will also be able to make phone calls on your behalf. Set up unofficial visits.

You can go on as many unofficial visits as you like. Pick some of your more serious choices and go and visit the campus and get in touch with the coach ahead of time and set up a meeting with them. It is also good to know when visiting colleges that you should try and visit the athletic office and see if the college coach is available for a personal introduction. Get the college coach to see you play.

Be aggressive and persistent in getting your game schedule in front of college coaches. This is the way you jump from the "maybe" pile to the "accepted" pile. Continue emailing and calling the college coach regarding your upcoming schedule. As tournaments get closer and game schedules are confirmed, send that schedule to the coach, noting time of kickoff, field number, your team's jersey color, and your jersey number.

Do not make the college coach have to look up information. If you place it in front of them, they are more likely to see you play. Communicate effectively with college coaches if there are any changes to your schedule and always follow up after each event. Take the SAT and ACT if you have not already done so. Register with the NCAA eligibility center. Be detailed and organized.

Keep a spreadsheet on each school, note when you emailed your bio, when you made phone calls, make notes on any conversations in person, on the phone, or over email and re-evaluate your top choices as the process moves along.

Your list of 15 to 25 schools should start to be more narrowed down to a top 5 to 10. Seniors should focus on school and grades... make sure you are improving your GPA and preparing for SATs. Meet with your school advisor to discuss colleges from an academic standpoint.

Once this has been finalized, start to apply for your chosen schools. Keep in touch with Admissions and college soccer coaches. Be punctual returning emails and phone calls. Fill out all Financial Aid documents as applicable. Make official visits. Try and get a feel for where you will fit in and what role you want to play. If you want to be an impact player who starts and gets minutes, then ask the coach if they see you as that player. If you are happy sitting on the bench and earning more time over the years, then you need to make that decision based on coaches' responses.

Pick the school that is the best fit for you academically, financially, athletically, and socially. Once your college choice has been made, do not back off your soccer preparation. The process does not stop once you have been accepted... your grades need to be maintained, and your fitness and soccer development needs to be continually worked on.

College coaches will send out summer fitness packets to help prepare players coming into their pre-season. It is important you follow that packet, and as an incoming freshman, you do extra preparation. Your Breakers Academy coach or College Liaison will be with you every step of the way in the process.

The PLAYER is accountable for the college process and not the PARENT or COACH.

The players who have the most success and the easiest process in their college selection have been the ones who have been self-motivated and aggressive in staying on top of things.

Finding the right college is a job in itself, after all the rewards for being persistent can be great. After all who doesn't want to go to the college of their dreams, play the sport they love at a high level, and maybe, just maybe, get some financial help along the way?

The Final Whistle

If you've read this far, you're clearly as passionate about the sport as I am. If you're brand new to the sport, here is a quick five-minute refresher that will get you through the first few months.

When you've been in the game for over four decades and had the opportunity to watch and talk with some of the best players and managers to have ever played, you learn things. Now it's my pleasure to share that knowledge.

Coaches who've seen me on TV often will ask "what was Sir Alex Ferguson like" or "were you intimidated by Zlatan Ibrahimovic," and the answers are, "charismatic" and "yes!"

I've also had the opportunity to mentor young coaches. That doesn't mean I've told them what to do, because every coach must follow their own path, but the following points are solid building blocks to creating the vision of you.

Start with a Vision

I've mentioned mission statement and core values at the start of the book, and I can't stress how important these two components are to creating the foundation of you.

Your vision is what you want people to see on the pitch and in your practice sessions. Does it show that you're a coach that wants to develop players both technically and tactically? Are you trying to teach them how to play the game and what does that game look like? This vision will guide you in your training sessions, and it is a vision that you'll share with your club, Technical Director, Athletic Director, and parents.

By having this long-term vision, it'll also protect you on the days when things don't quite go so well. It helped me when my U11 girls took a 6-0 pasting the other day, and my parents were starting to lose their minds. All I had to do was send out a quick email, and everyone was back in the fold.

Your Coaching Identity

Where we come from and how we've learned to coach has a huge imprint on us whether we like it or not. I know the English coaches get labeled with a "long ball merchant" sticker and that's hard to shrug when I love to see a full back clip a ball down the line to a flying winger, who whips in a first time cross for a striker to batter home as opposed to a 25 pass build up.

However, your style, attitude, charisma, and personality have a huge impact on the players you coach. Obviously, I'm not the same coach in terms of delivery for U11 girls and Cal FC, but the message remains consistent.

I want my players to be fabulous decision makers because that is the ultimate barometer between good and bad players, but my number one responsibility I feel is helping my players develop a love of the game.

Ask anyone I've ever coached if "Nick loves the game of soccer," and the answer is yes. Administrators, parents, and players all know exactly what my coaching identity is and it comes from a place of deep love.

Watch the Best

When you've stood on the sidelines and observed Sir Alex Ferguson, Jose Mourinho, and Carlo Ancelotti work you can't help but understand the way to run a practice, patrol the technical area, and dominate a press conference.

Yes, I get that 99.9% of us will never work at that level with the quality and caliber of players they have at their disposal, but that doesn't mean to say you can't work **like** them or imitate the way they go about their business.

There is nothing to stop you from calling up your local MLS, USL, NASL team, or your local college and ask if you can come and watch a training session... the worst they can say is no!

When you're at the training session, suck it all in. From the moment the players, training staff, and coach hit the field. Look at everything the coach does – especially his interaction with the players. What is the coach focusing on... is it technical or tactical?

Are set pieces addressed from both sides of the ball, attacking and defending? What's the body language of the coach... is he relaxed, laid back or is in full throttle and in his players' faces? You have to be able to answer those questions, because you need to be able to recognize qualities in you that will work with your club and players.

When I first started as a coach, I was Cesar Monetti, who was known as El Flaco (the slim one) who coached Argentina to the World Cup title in 1978. I thought he was cool personified as he sat on the bench chain-smoking cigarettes, never flustered and always immaculate in a pressed shirt and pants.

The chain-smoking aside, I liked the way he impassively watched the game, like a grand chess master. However, I soon discovered that wouldn't work with U15 boys and had to develop a more Sir Alex Ferguson-like presence that demanded and cajoled performances.

Whoever it is, though, be that person until you figure out who you are. Today I'd like to think I have many qualities that include a little Menotti and a little Fergie, but ultimately a lot of me.

Managing People

As a soccer coach, you're more than X's and O's. You have to manage your fellow coaches, assistant, and parents. I've spoken at length about parents elsewhere in the book, however in this era of pay-to-play you better know your players and parents really well.

The sooner you figure out what buttons to push and levers to pull, you'll have happy parents and players all moving in the direction of your vision and values. I've mentioned communication many times, and I'll mention it again. Do yourself a favor and over communicate. Make people sick of your emails.

I recently benched both my striker and center-back on my boys U17 team who started the previous 10 games, and I let them both know why. I also explained to their parents why I was doing this and the result was no emails or phone calls from parents who were pissed off because their child wasn't playing.

And if you're feeling bold and confident in your management style, invite the parents into a post-game huddle after a big performance. That is worth its weight in gold.

Integrity

Keep it, keep it, and keep it! I think there is a saying somewhere that it takes a lifetime to build and only a few seconds to destroy it!

I honestly believe that the game of soccer and everything that surrounds it is a microcosm of life. There are so many lessons that we can take away from the game and make part of our lifestyle.

I've been incredibly lucky and have participated in this game from every conceivable level, and I hope that the advice and anecdotes can help you through the tough times when they do come rolling around.

Above all, keep a "growth" mindset going in your coaching career. There is never one way of coaching and the more exposure you give yourself to different styles of soccer and different ways of teaching, the better-rounded you become.

My goal has always been for soccer to become the number one sport in this amazing country we call America. Yes, the competition from other sports is intense, but nothing beats the freedom players experience playing this game.

It has always been a player's game, and we as coaches are here to make sure that that will always be the case. The players are number one, we are number two.

Lastly, I'd like to say that I'll always be here for you. If you need me, there is always a way to get in contact. Whether through Facebook or Twitter, make an effort to reach out, and I'll get back to you because we're in this thing together.

The last thing I'll give you on this epic journey is my alphabet soup. This took forever and if I'm honest seems to change every day but on this particular day, it looked like this...

My A to Z

Attitude: Your attitude will become your players' attitudes. Everything you do will in one way or another rub off on them in small and large ways. I know it is almost impossible to have a great attitude all the time, what with annoying parents and referees that seem intent on cheating you, but keep calm and carry on.

Ball: Nothing keeps a player's interest alive more than the ball. Make sure every player brings their well inflated, size appropriate ball to practice and games. You can't be a player unless you have a ball.

Crossing: Nothing will drive you crazier than watching your players trying to cross the ball without turning their hips. It's simple physics. Your hips have to point towards your target, or the ball will go straight out of play.

Decisions: Quite simply the difference between a good player and a bad player. Preach good decision making all day, and you may end up with a player or a group of players that take the world by storm.

Ego: No matter how successful you get always keep that ego of yours in check. Whenever parents congratulate you on a win, make sure to deflect it to your players because when you lose, which we all eventually do, you can then look at the players!

Fun: Yes, it's so corny, but unless we're playing this game for money, the ultimate goal for coaches and players alike is to have fun. Be prepared to make fun of yourself and the insanity that this game sometimes brings to the most bizarre situations.

Goals: The lifeblood of the game. Every practice session you have must involve scoring goals because nothing beats the feeling of seeing a ball hit the back of the net.

Hugs: I know I've told you to watch your hands, however, nothing beats the hugs of a great victory.

Inspire: As a coach, you have an amazing position and the ability to change lives. Relish that role and make it your goal to inspire the players you work with to come to every practice and game with lots of enthusiasm, hard work, and the desire to be a great teammate.

Juggling: Every player under the age of fifteen should be juggling a ball every day for at least ten minutes. It provides multiple touches, develops balance, and allows players to hone their creativity. As a coach, encourage competition between your players and don't let kids use their hands to start the ball going unless absolutely necessary. Also, don't sweat the kids if the ball bounces; get them to keep going with BOTH feet.

Knowledge: Never stop learning. Watch YouTube for new and cool drills and exercises. Read the latest coaching manuals, listen to peers, and if you can, take coaching courses. You may have all the answers already, but it never hurts to listen to new voices. I've found that coaching courses validate what I've been trying to do and that in itself is worth the price of admission.

Love: The single most important component that every player and coach must possess. We have been given this wonderful game that for the most part tortures and befuddles us, and it's in these moments that our love must be at its strongest. I have such great memories of wins, however it's in the toughest losses that I've preached to my players that this is why we love the game... because it's so unfair!

Money: Where else but the US of A could you make a decent living coaching a game that you love at the youth level...the answer is nowhere. America...what a country!

Notice: Be aware of your surroundings. Think of player safety and once you have that sorted, look at your players, and notice what they are doing. Do not let anything slide in terms of technique, tactics, or behavior. When you're on the job, do not get distracted by anything, because you've got a lot on your plate. Your team, your opponents, subs, parents, refs, you name it, I want you to notice it.

Organization: I may have mentioned this earlier in the book, but reality is perception. If you are organized, people will automatically think you're a good coach and will give you the benefit of the doubt when things go south. Organization takes an extra ten to fifteen minutes, and while it feels like a pain in the butt, it'll save you hours down the line.

Penalties: Practice them, they win games.

Questions: The only way you can really improve as a coach is to keep asking questions. No one knows it all, although you'll meet some coaches who think they do. Questions are powerful, and while there are some truly stupid questions, there is never a stupid question about soccer.

Referees: Love them, hate them, they have the hardest job in soccer. What I would request you to do is try and make friends with them, share a joke and realize that 99.9% of them are not trying to cheat you, and get you the sack. Soccer is such a subjective game, and we can all see decisions in so many ways, however if we can teach our players to respect referees by our own actions, we'll have done the world a favor and made our planet a better place.

Scoring: Our players watch professionals and when a pro scores, crazy things happen, and they lose their minds and rip off their shirts earning themselves a yellow card (red if they've already been cautioned). Our players imitate the professionals, so give a kid some slack if they whip off their shirt in that frenzied moment, just let them know that that was their "one time" for the season.

Training: Every session is valuable, however, I know that it's almost impossible to bring 100% of you every single time, but make sure that even when you are running on fumes, at least one of your players gets something positive out of a training session.

Understanding: Every player is different. You cannot treat everyone the same. It is vital for your "growth" as a coach and a person that you take the time to develop and understand where your players are coming from socially, physically, and mentally.

Victory: I remember reading Sir Alex Ferguson's book called "Leadership." He said he barely got to enjoy the wins because as soon as the trophy was lifted, he was already thinking about the next one. Sir Alex Ferguson was a one off, and his success will never be replicated. You, on the other hand, should savor every moment because you don't know when they'll come around again.

Whining: You've heard them many times... your opposite number with a running commentary of complaints about the ref, your team, the parents. Don't be that coach.

X-factor: If you're lucky enough to have that player, the one player that drives you completely mad but at the same time can do things with a ball that mere mortals can only dream about. Nurture them and find out what makes them tick because it's these players, the special players, that bring a lot of joy to the beautiful game.

Yellow cards: For players and coaches, there are good yellows cards, and there are bad yellow cards. Learn to recognize which is which because there are lessons to be learned.

Zero chance: As soccer becomes the biggest sport in America, the haters are going to hate, but there is zero chance we are going anywhere. Enjoy this ride, it's going to be a blast.

Sample Forms/Letters

Sample Waiver

Player Registration Form & Waiver

PLAYER NAME (PRINT)_____

BIRTH DATE_____

STREET ADDRESS_____

CITY_____ZIP_____

EMAIL ADDRESS (PRINT)_____

HOME PHONE_____CELL PHONE_____

PARENTS' NAMES_____

DOCTOR_____DOCTOR PHONE_____

INSURANCE CARRIER_____POLICY #_____

MEDICAL CONDITIONS/ALLERGIES_____

In consideration of the benefits derived, and in view of the fact that Mar Vista Football Club (MVFC) is a non-profit organization, and that the participation with MVFC is voluntary, and recognizing that the sport of soccer carries certain risk and that every normal precaution will be taken to ensure the safety and being of my son/daughter, named above, in all activities of MVFC, I agree to his/her participation and waive all claims against MVFC, including claims against Coaches, Managers, Club Officials, Agents, Sponsors or other representatives of MVFC

SIGNATURE OF PARENT OR GUARDIAN_____

DATE OF SIGNATURE_____

Sample Medical Release Form

This form must be completed for each soccer player/participant under 18-years of age.

ORGANIZATION

MEDICAL RELEASE FORM

PLAYER'S NAME: _____

ADDRESS: _____

CITY: _____ STATE: _____

ZIP CODE: _____

BIRTHDATE: _____ GENDER: _____

DATE OF MOST RECENT TETANUS SHOT: _____

ANY KNOWN ALLERGIES (especially to medications):

_____

_____

MEDICAL CONDITIONS:

_____

_____

PRIMARY MEDICAL INSURANCE COMPANY: _____

POLICY NUMBER: _____
GROUP OR TYPE NUMBER: _____

PLAYER'S PRIMARY PHYSICIAN'S NAME: _____

PHYSICIAN'S PHONE NUMBER: _____

PARENT OR LEGAL GUARDIAN NAME: _____

HOME PHONE: _____

CELL PHONE: _____

WORK PHONE: _____

IN MY ABSENCE, ANY ONE OF THE FOLLOWING PEOPLE, IN THE ORDER IDENTIFIED BELOW, IS HEREBY DESIGNATED TO ACT ON MY BEHALF:

1. SECONDARY CONTACT NAME: _____

HOME PHONE: _____

CELL PHONE: _____

WORK PHONE: _____

2. COACH: _____

3. ASSISTANT COACH/TEAM MANAGER: _____

4. TEAM PARENT: _____

5. A REPRESENTATIVE OF THE ORGANIZATION WHERE MY CHILD IS PLAYING: _____

6. A REPRESENTATIVE OF THE TOURNAMENT WHERE MY CHILD IS PLAYING: _____

In my absence, I hereby give my consent and permission for medical transportation and to have a paramedic and/or duly licensed Doctor of Medicine and/or duly licensed Doctor of Dentistry provide my child or legal guardian, a minor identified as "Player's Name" above, with any and all medical assistance or treatment deemed necessary in the event of an accident, injury, or sudden illness. Further, I authorize admission to any hospital or medical facility for such treatment, including diagnostic procedures performed by licensed technicians or nurses. I authorize the hospital or medical facility to dispose of any specimens or tissue as appropriate. This release is effective until my arrival and its revoked by me. I agree to be responsible financially for the cost of each transportation, assistance or treatment.

SIGNATURE: _____

DATE: _____

Welcome to the Team

Dear Player:

Thank you for participating in the 2016 – 2017, (team name) soccer tryouts. As you know, only 15-18 players were selected out those who tried out. Unfortunately, you have not been selected as a member of this year's team.

I appreciate your hard work and dedication during tryouts. I encourage you to keep working and to try out again next year at (team name). It is not uncommon for players who did not make the team one year to keep working on their skills and make the team the following year. There are many ways to improve your skills such as playing in the other organized leagues or by attending one of the many soccer camps that are offered in our area.

One of my most difficult responsibilities of being a coach is making decisions about who will make the team. We take this responsibility very seriously. As a person who has been cut from a team before, I know how you are feeling at this moment.

Please talk to your parents about times in their lives when they have worked hard for something that did not end up going the way they hoped. Sooner or later this happens to everyone. I want to remind you that there will be girls/boys playing high school soccer this year that received the same letter that you received today. Keep working on your game and good luck next year.

Sincerely,
Coach Webster

Not Making the Team

Dear Player: Lionel Messi

Thank you for participating in the 2016 – 2017, (team name) soccer tryouts. As you know, only 15-18 players were selected out those who tried out. Unfortunately, you have not been selected as a member of this year's team.

I appreciate your hard work and dedication during tryouts. I encourage you to keep working and to try out again next year at (team name). It is not uncommon for players who did not make the team one year to keep working on their skills and make the team the following year. There are many ways to improve your skills such as playing in the other organized leagues or by attending one of the many soccer camps that are offered in our area.

One of my most difficult responsibilities of being a coach is making decisions about who will make the team. We take this responsibility very seriously. As a person who has been cut from a team before, I know how you are feeling at this moment.

Please talk to your parents about times in their lives when they have worked hard for something that did not end up going the way they hoped. Sooner or later this happens to everyone. I want to remind you that there will be girls/boys playing high school soccer this year that received the same letter that you received today. Keep working on your game and good luck next year.

Sincerely,
Coach Webster